Managing Competitive Crisis
Strategic Choice and the Reform of Workrules

The most controversial aspect of institutional regeneration in North America and Europe over the last twenty years has been the restructuring of labour relations. Media attention has been drawn to the resulting claims of excess employer power; however, supporters of union reform point to the recent spate of strikes in Western Europe as the predicament that the UK has escaped.

In this timely monograph Martyn Wright examines how competitive crisis affected the management of work relations in Britain between 1979 and 1991. Using longitudinal analysis and a wealth of case study material from companies and employers' associations, the study moves beyond the normal cross-sectional survey to reveal a complex pattern of procedural and substantive rule change, and illustrates considerable variation in the context to which competitive crisis was harnessed by employers to generate an ongoing momentum for change. *Managing Competitive Crisis* is a must for students of organisational change.

Martyn Wright is a Lecturer in Industrial Relations and Organisational Behaviour at the University of Warwick.

Cambridge Studies in Management

Editors
WILLIAM BROWN, *University of Cambridge*
JOHN CHILD, *University of Cambridge*
ANTHONY HOPWOOD, *London School of Economics*
PAUL WILLMAN, *London Business School*

Cambridge Studies in Management focuses on the human and organisational aspects of management. It covers the areas of organisation theory and behaviour, strategy and business policy, the organisational and social aspects of accounting, personnel and human resource management, industrial relations and industrial sociology.

The series aims for high standards of scholarship and seeks to publish the best among original theoretical and empirical research; innovative contributions to advancing understanding in the area; and books which synthesise and/or review the best of current research, and aim to make the work published in specialist journals more widely accessible.

The books are intended for an international audience among specialists in universities and business schools, for undergraduate and MBA students, and also for a wider readership among business practitioners and trade unionists.

For a list of titles in this series, see end of book.

Managing Competitive Crisis

Strategic Choice and the Reform of Workrules

Martyn Wright

CAMBRIDGE
UNIVERSITY PRESS

PUBLISHED BY THE PRESS SYNDICATE OF THE UNIVERSITY OF CAMBRIDGE
The Pitt Building, Trumpington Street, Cambridge CB2 1RP, United Kingdom

CAMBRIDGE UNIVERSITY PRESS
The Edinburgh Building, Cambridge CB2 2RU, United Kingdom
  http://www.cup.cam.ac.uk
40 West 20th Street, New York, NY 10011-4211, USA   http://www.cup.org
10 Stamford Road, Oakleigh, Melbourne 3166, Australia

First published 2000

Printed in the United Kingdom at the University Press, Cambridge

Typeset in Times NR 10/12 pt   [SE]

A catalogue record for this book is available from the British Library

Library of Congress Cataloguing in Publication data

Wright, Martyn.
Managing competitive crisis: strategic choice and the reform of
workrules / Martyn Wright.
      p.   cm. – (Cambridge studies in management)
Includes bibliographical references.
ISBN 0 521 64005 9 (hardback)
1. Industrial relations – Great Britain.   2. Competition – Great
Britain.   3. Industrial management – Great Britain.   I. Title.
II. Series.
HD8391.W75   2000
331′.0941–dc21   99–20174   CIP

ISBN 0 521 64005 9 hardback

Contents

Figures

Tables

Acknowledgments

Although only one person is credited with authorship, this book is the product of collaboration with many people. Stephen Dunn originally employed me as his research assistant at the London School of Economics, during which time we collected much of the data on which this book is based. Numerous other individuals have, at various times, commented on the text in part or whole. I thank Paul Edwards, John Roberts, Hugh Whittaker, and present and former colleagues at the Industrial Relations Research Unit, University of Warwick, Management Studies Group, University of Cambridge, and Centre for Economic Performance, London School of Economics. The profoundest debt is owed to William Brown, for whose supervision I have nothing but thanks.

Abbreviations

CLIRS	Warwick Company-Level Industrial Relations Survey
EA	employers' association
HRM	human resource management
TQM	total quality management
UMA	union membership agreements
WIRS	Workplace Industrial Relations Survey

1   Introduction

The key theme of this book is how economic crisis shaped the management of workrules in unionised companies in Britain between 1979 and 1991. During this period, many of the advanced industrialised countries experienced product market collapse and labour market slump. Britain endured an especially harsh recession in the early 1980s. Commentators have argued that these competitive shocks weakened the collective organisation of labour on the shopfloor, and engendered the radical restructuring of working practices in unionised companies. But there has been less attention to the processes by which such change took place, and in particular to the interplay between economic pressures, the 'strategic choices' made by managers, and the pattern of change to formal rule structures and informal practices at the workplace.

These themes are explored through a comparison of fifty highly unionised companies in Britain in 1979 and 1991. Semi-structured interviews were undertaken with senior personnel managers in each company in both years. Reference will also be made to a panel of fifteen employers' associations, interviewed in 1979 and again in 1990. The comparative advantage of these data is that they highlight the broad patterns and specific processes of reform. The study aspires neither to the richness of the detailed case study nor to the coverage of the large-scale questionnaire survey. Rather, the aim is to explore the process of adjustment in a panel of organisations which have in common strong labour organisation and deeply entrenched collective-bargaining institutions.

This first chapter is set out in four further sections which examine the nature of economic crisis in Britain and the other advanced economies; economic crisis and industrial relations reform; strategic choice and industrial relations change; and strategic choice under crisis conditions.

Economic crisis in Britain and the other advanced economies

Economic crisis has afflicted much of the Western industrialised world in the past twenty years, most especially the decentralised market-driven economies, such as Britain and the United States. Between the end of the Second World War and the middle of the 1970s, many of the advanced economies enjoyed historically high rates of unbroken economic growth. Compared to the slumps of the inter-war era, demand for manufactured goods and services was buoyant, unemployment was low and skilled labour was scarce. In most Western industrialised countries, trade union membership was rising and penetrating into previously unorganised sectors of the economy and into traditionally non-union occupational groups.

Since the middle of the 1970s the Western economies have suffered a sustained economic downturn. National economies have experienced lengthy periods of recession, while unemployment has risen to and persists at historically high rates. These trends are in part a consequence of the globalisation of competition, a process which has accelerated in the past twenty years. The range of product lines and branded goods has expanded, and products markets have become further segmented. With advances in microprocessor technology, there has been a quickening in the frequency with which products and services are re-specified, and production systems are reconfigured.

In response to the failure of the economy, governments in several countries, including the United States, have attempted to 'deregulate' labour markets, and to weaken the bargaining position of trade unions. In few countries was the economic crisis as severe, or the reframing of employment law as marked, as in Britain. For much of the 1950s and 1960s, the British political economy was characterised by Keynesian demand management to sustain high rates of consumption together with low rates of unemployment (for reviews, see Dunn 1979, MacInness 1987). To this might be added a preference for 'voluntarism', or free collective bargaining between employees and trade unions, in which the role of employment law was largely confined to setting a 'minimum floor' of wage and health and safety standards. This system came to be associated with the post-war economic boom conditions of high output and scarce labour which prevailed until the early 1970's.

Concern at Britain's relatively slow economic growth, balance of payments difficulties and persistent inflation grew during the 1960s. Trade unions and the voluntarist industrial relations system were considered a factor in the sluggish rate of growth, so much so that the Donovan Commission was established in 1965. The report of the Commission (Donovan 1968) argued that tight labour markets and expanding product markets had enabled groups of workers on the shopfloor to exert bargaining pressure over supervisors and junior management. The outcome was a disjuncture between the 'formal' system of collective bargaining at industry level, and the 'informal' system at the workplace. The unofficial and fragmented nature of bargaining on the shopfloor led to wage 'drift', or a disparity between rates stipulated in national agreements and those paid on the shopfloor, together with 'restrictive practices' including overmanning and systematic overtime, and unconstitutional or 'wildcat' strike action (Dunn 1979: 10). Donovan's prescription, consistent with the voluntarist ethos, was the extension of the system of formalised collective bargaining to the workplace, and the development of written, comprehensive collective agreements at this level.

With the Industrial Relations Act 1971, passed by the Heath government, came an initial incursion into the voluntarist 'space' (Dunn 1979: 1). The Act required trade unions to register to preserve their immunity from liability for inducing breaching of contract. It also provided for a mandatory 'cooling-off' period, as well as compulsory balloting, in the case of 'unfair industrial practices'. Collective agreements were also assumed to be legally enforceable contracts, unless the parties stipulated otherwise.

By the middle of the 1970s, the trade-off between inflation and unemployment upon which Keynesian demand management was founded appeared to be breaking down, and conditions of 'stagflation' prevailed – persistent price inflation combined with low economic growth. Between 1974 and 1975, unemployment increased from 0.6 million to above 1 million, while inflation also rose from 9.3 per cent in 1973 to over 26 per cent in 1975 (Dunn 1979: 26). The Labour government turned to the Social Contract, in which union wage restraint was traded for the repeal of the Industrial Relations Act 1971 and a new employment law framework, along with measures to boost demand and reduce unemployment. The Social Contract began to unravel in 1977–8, with union leaders increasingly unwilling or unable to impose wage restraint upon their members. With it, the Labour government turned to measures to restrict the money supply, in an attempt to combat inflation.

For the incoming Conservative government in 1979, tight monetary policy was one of the cornerstones of its economic policy. Interest rates were raised, in an attempt to halt the growth of cash and credit. As the value of the pound soared, and exports became more expensive and imports cheaper, the British economy moved sharply into recession. The fall in output and employment in Britain in the early 1980s was much greater than in the other industrialised economies (see Table 1.1). British manufacturing output fell by 17 per cent between 1979 and 1981, and by 9 per cent in 1980 alone. Product market collapse was accompanied by labour market slump. The manufacturing and processing sectors, where union organisation was at its strongest, were affected by job shedding on a scale unprecedented in the post-war period. Seasonally adjusted unemployment increased. Between 1975 and 1978, unemployment averaged just above 1,000,000. From 1979 to 1982, this figure averaged approximately 2,000,000, and then between 1983 and 1986, more than 3,000,000.

Table 1.1 *Maximum two-year percentage decline after 1979*

Country	Output	Employment
UK	3.5	5.7
US	0.4	(0.4)
France	(1.6)	1.3
Germany	0.4	3.2
Italy	(0.7)	(0.6)
Sweden	(0.5)	0.9
EEC	(0.6)	2.1

Source: Layard and Nickell (1989: 13)
Figures in brackets indicate increase.

The Thatcher government also profoundly altered the legal and political status of organised labour. The government took an aggressive stance towards bargaining with public sector unions, the outcome of which was a series of industrial disputes in the public sector, most notably in the coal mining industry in 1984–5 but also in water, rail transport, local government and secondary and higher education. Union recognition and the right to be a member of a trade union were withdrawn at GCHQ, the government intelligence communications headquarters. Government also refused to condemn employer action to derecognise unions in the print industry, as with the Stockport Messenger and News International industrial disputes.

Far-reaching changes were made to the framework of trade union and employment law between 1979 and 1991 (for reviews, sees Brown, Deakin and Ryan 1997, Dickens and Hall 1995, Dunn and Metcalf 1996). The closed shop, whereby union membership is made a requirement in order to obtain ('pre-entry' shop) or retain ('post-entry' shop) employment, was made legally unenforceable. The scope for unions to organise effective industrial action was narrowed. Trade union immunity for inducing breach of contract was withdrawn for strike action other than with the workers' own employer and at their own place of work. Immunity was also denied where the action takes place without a postal ballot of union members.

In addition to the magnitude of the changes in the political economy, their unanticipated nature also denotes this period as one of crisis. The collapse in corporate profitability came against a backdrop of a thirty-year period of relative stability and prosperity. Several major companies, such as the construction group BICC, recorded their first operating loss in the post-war era within the first three years of the Thatcher administration. The early 1980s also reversed long-standing trends in the UK labour market, such as the extension of union membership to traditionally non-union sectors of the economy, including private services, and to historically unorganised occupational groups such as white-collar, clerical, supervisory and managerial employees. The 1977–9 period marked a post-war high not only in aggregate union membership and union density, but also in the percentage of employees covered by collective agreements, and in the total number of days lost through industrial action. Cognitive psychologists commonly argue that perceivers' expectations of the future are informed by their experience of the recent past (e.g., Reger 1990). Any expectations of a continued and rising tide of trade union and labour influence into the 1980s were quickly confounded.

Economic crisis and industrial relations reform

The main question posed by the present study is how the economic and political shifts outlined above impacted upon the institutional framework of industrial relations in unionised companies. Fortunately, several large-scale surveys were conducted in the 1980s, which offer detailed and comprehensive data on industrial relations change. These include the Workplace Industrial Relations Survey (WIRS), which examined some 2,000 establishments with twenty-five or more employees in 1980 (Daniel and Millward 1983), 1984 (Millward and Stevens 1986) and 1990 (Millward et al. 1992); the Warwick Company Level Industrial Relations Survey (CLIRS), of 143 companies in 1985 and 176 companies in 1992 (Marginson et al. 1993); the survey by Gregg and Yates (1991) of industrial relations practices in 558 UK companies for the periods 1980–4 and 1985–9; and Edwards' (1987) survey of 229 factory managers in plants with 250 or more employees. Finally, there is the earlier company-level survey of manufacturing enterprises by Brown and his colleagues (Brown 1981).

Evidence suggests that the combination of product market pressures, increased unemployment and legal restrictions on the organising ability of trade unions led to widespread restructuring of work practices (Metcalf 1989, 1994, Oulton 1995). As Layard and Nickel (1989: 13) argued: 'the collapse in output and employment, accompanied as it was by an enormous rise in closures and bankruptcies . . . gave both workers and management little alternative but to increase productivity or go under.' Fear of bankruptcy, it is argued, disciplined employers into confronting over-manning and union job controls (Metcalf 1989: 19). Legislative change, combined with fear of redundancy, left unions less capable of opposing such changes and workers more inclined to comply with managerial demands (Oulton 1995, Metcalf 1989). Substantive change in unionised workplaces was commonly negotiated through collective-bargaining procedures. Where unions proved to be a material obstacle to restructuring, management were increasingly prepared to terminate union recognition in whole or in part, and to refute union membership agreements. These changes in union status may have signalled to employees a greater assertiveness on the part of management, together with the need to work harder, which may have been a factor in raising labour productivity in unionised establishments (Gregg, Machin and Metcalf 1993).

Such an argument implies a measure of continuity in collective-bargaining arrangements, for which there is some supporting evidence. The large majority of establishments that recognised trade unions in 1984 continued to do so in 1990 (Gregg and Yates 1991). Shop steward organisation in union companies remained little changed, although the total number of stewards had fallen in line with the total employed in the unionised sector. Procedures for industrial disputes and individual employee grievances also remained largely intact. While there is evidence of continued union presence in the majority of establishments that were unionised in 1979, this has been accompanied by widespread restructuring of collective-bargaining arrangements. The scope of issues which were covered by collective bargaining contracted. Union derecognition, while confined to a minority of enterprises, became more common. WIRS found that 9 per cent of the panel of trading sector workplaces reported the complete withdrawal of collective-bargaining rights between 1984 and 1990 (Millward *et al.* 1992: 75). Even where collective-bargaining procedures were retained, the level of bargaining had frequently been decentralised away from the multi-employer or corporate level. Walsh (1993) interviewed personnel managers in eighteen large, private-sector organisations in 1990 about their pay-setting arrangements. Nine companies had withdrawn from multi-employer bargaining or had decentralised collective bargaining in the 1980s (1993: 413). But the devolution of pay bargaining was often accompanied by the corporate centre monitoring or directly controlling pay levels in subsidiaries and establishments, to minimise the scope for pay leapfrogging.

Perhaps most notable was the reported decline in the presence of the closed shop, which has long been considered a symbol of union power (McCarthy 1963, Dunn and Gennard 1984). The pre-entry closed shop especially has been associated with union power to drive up the relative pay of workers covered by it (Metcalf 1993). An expansion in the coverage of the closed shop was registered in the 1970s, as closed shop arrangements extended to previously uncovered sectors such as food, drink and tobacco, clothing and footwear, transport and communications, the public utilities, and into non-manual occupational groups (Dunn and Gennard 1984: 15–16). These 'soft' closed shops were more likely to result from managerially sponsored procedural reform, than were the 'hard' closed shops in industries such as engineering, print and port transport, which had been imposed upon management, or in which management had acquiesced in order to promote stability and workplace order (Dunn and Gennard 1984: 41–55). In line with legislative change, WIRS shows a steep fall in the incidence of the closed shop in the 1980s. Compulsory union-ism became 'far less numerous', diminishing from 20 per cent of establish-ments in 1984, to 4 per cent in 1990 for manual workers, and from 9 per cent to 1 per cent for non-manuals.

While collective-bargaining procedures may have remained extant in the majority of union establishments, there is evidence to suggest that manage-ment were increasingly able to define the bargaining agenda and to secure their preferred outcomes in negotiations. Morris and Wood (1991) inter-viewed personnel managers at a range of levels in fifteen large, private-sector organisations that were surveyed in the first CLIRS (Marginson *et al.* 1988). Morris and Wood (1991) found considerable continuity in pro-cedural arrangements, such as union recognition, bargaining structures, consultation arrangements and shop steward facilities. But management had been changing the way that institutions worked. Management was becoming more confident about gaining 'what they wanted' from bargain-ing (1991: 269): 'In all but two of the [thirteen] unionised firms in our sample, managers said they took the initiative in negotiations more now' (1991: 270). Even where the number of shop stewards had remained unchanged, management had frequently attempted to reduce their influence, using methods such as limiting the number of shopfloor meetings allowed in work time and returning full time stewards to their work roles (1991: 271).

Storey (1992) finds that attacks on procedure in his fifteen case study companies were rare. But management had 'seized the initiative' and were more inclined to take an aggressive stance towards unions without having an agenda to replace them (1992: 77 and 246). Gregg and Yates (1991) report managerial perceptions of union strength. In what they admit to be a crude test, in the period 1984–9, 57 per cent of respondents felt that unions had become weaker, as against 7 per cent who felt that unions had become stronger. Case studies, such as in the coal industry after the 1984 strike, indicate that management were becoming better able to push through changes to working practices which increased labour productivity (Richardson and Wood 1989).

There is also evidence of widespread work restructuring, particularly of an attack on union job controls over effort and output, upon demarcation lines between labour of different crafts or skills, the introduction of new technology and the reduction of staffing levels (e.g., Metcalf 1989, Storey and Sisson 1993). Dunn and Wright (1994) examined the contents of fifty collective agreements in 1979 and 1990. They found that procedural indices, such as the scope of union recognition, disputes procedures and the administrative facilities that were granted to shop stewards, had remained largely intact. Substantive indices, such as productivity clauses, job structures and flexibility agreements had been much more extensively overhauled. However, there is little evidence to suggest that a more fundamental redesign of jobs has occurred. Storey and Sisson (1993) note that profound alterations in job content have been rare and changes are more likely to have taken the form of 'financially driven cost reductions' (1993: 34–5). 'Advanced' teamworking systems, the core of which are self-governing work groups, remain confined to a small minority of establishments (Geary 1995).

In summary, the competitive crisis of the early 1980s forced management to uproot union job controls and to implement more efficient forms of work organisation, while legislative reforms reduced the ability of trade union to resist these changes. Much of this change was negotiated through collective-bargaining procedures, although such procedures had often been decentralised away from the multi-employer and corporate level. Closed shop arrangements had commonly been rescinded, while in a minority of establishments, union recognition had been partly or completely withdrawn.

The context and processes of industrial relations change

In addition to the above broad developments, there is also evidence that management industrial relations policies and styles became increasingly diverse in the 1980s. Certain authors have argued that the Donovan model of formalised, decentralised collective bargaining may have come to dominate management thinking in unionised companies in the late 1970s. Dunn (1993) argues that management 'got incorporated' by Donovan logic, which stunted their ambition and unionised their imagination. There is certainly evidence to support such a view. Written collective-bargaining agreements, including grievance and disputes procedures, became more common at establishment level in the 1970s (Sisson and Brown 1983, Storey 1983). Shop steward organisation, such as formal entitlements to time off work and access to office facilities, was strengthened. There was, as noted above, a broadening in the coverage of the closed shop (Dunn and Gennard 1984). Storey (1980) suggests that the range of issues that were subject to joint workplace control expanded during the 1970s, which would be consistent with the formalisation of shopfloor procedures. These developments may have been especially well represented among the present panel of firms, which was determined in 1979 by high union membership and likely operation of a closed shop. It was to companies such as these, with strong collective organisation, to which Donovan primarily directed its reform proposals.

By the early 1990s, Dunn (1993) argues, management had 'deincorporated' itself from Donovan, and a 'more diverse pattern' of management policy was evident, with companies having embarked on widely differing courses of reform. Others detect a similar fracturing of personnel management orthodoxy. Purcell and Ahlstrand's (1994) study of multi-divisional companies (1994: 209) found a shift away from the previously numerically dominant policy which centred upon formalised collective bargaining – what they term 'bargained constitutionalism'. Companies were turning to a whole host of other policies. One popular route was towards a 'sophisticated consultative' policy, which combines a union presence with a more developmental approach to employees (1994: 197 and 213). Others were shifting towards a 'traditional' style of cost minimisation and labour subordination, or towards the 'sophisticated human relations' style, in which non-unionism is allied with 'commitment-empowerment' employee management.

Storey (1992) observed a 'retreat from proceduralism', along with a 'welter of initiatives' and a 'bewildering variety of approaches' (1992: 2). Management were experimenting with schemes which included 'an emphasis upon adaptability, direct communication with employees, "managerial leadership", and the moulding of a more tractable employee stock' (1992: 77). These initiatives were usually placed alongside existing collective bargaining and employee representation arrangements. Ahlstrand's (1990) study of the Fawley refinery shows how management turned away from its long-standing policy of negotiating formal productivity agreements, following their 'obvious failure', in favour of union derecognition, and the introduction of personal employee contracts with individual appraisal and reward.

The factories in Scott's (1994) three case studies had started to follow quite different labour relations policies, with the biscuit works remaining committed to Donovan-style pluralism, while the frozen food works had reorganised production into autonomous teams of workers. At the chocolate works, management had chosen to introduce single status, extend the incentive payments scheme to the shopfloor, eliminate direct supervision and transfer tasks such as minor maintenance duties and quality checking to production operatives.

Strategic choice and industrial relations change

Accounting for the greater diversity of industrial relations policies and styles apparent by the early 1990s is plainly fundamental to any assessment of the overall pattern of change. Perhaps the most influential studies to have addressed these processes are the US 'strategic choice' studies (Kochan, Katz and McKersie 1986, Capelli 1984, Kochan et al. 1984). Examining the competitive pressures faced by large US enterprises in the late 1970s and early 1980s, Kochan and his colleagues argued that the major industrial relations actors – government, unions and, especially, management – must be seen as active agents with a degree of choice over their preferences and behaviour. Actors exercise choice at three levels of the system (Table 1.2): over long-term strategic business policy and human resource issues, such as investment, plant location and new technology; over collective bargaining and personnel policy, such as personnel and negotiation strategies; and over workplace relations, such as supervisory style, worker participation and work organisation. Decisions are 'strategic' in that they bind the three levels of the system together.

Kochan *et al.* (1986) advance a link between the external environment and the institutional structure of firm-level industrial relations (Figure 1). This link is mediated by the values and strategies of the main actors, and by their history and current structures. Thus a destabilising incident, such as aggressive market moves by competitor firms, sets in motion a stream of business and industrial relations decisions (Kochan *et al.* 1984: 22). A firm must first decide upon its commitment to its existing lines of business, whether it wishes to continue to compete in these sectors or to withdraw from them. There then follow a series of 'competitive strategy' decisions, such as whether to compete on the basis of low cost, high quality or to be a niche player; such considerations frame downstream industrial relations issues, including collective-bargaining priorities.

Capelli (1984) shows for the airline industry that following deregulation, carriers pursued quite differing competitive strategies, and varied in their decisions to compete in the heavily contested, high volume trunk routes, or to avoid competition by concentrating upon the more sheltered, low-volume regional routes. These business decisions were informed by the carrier's financial position and available aircraft and by management's view of the market and the goals of their own firm (1984: 321). Such matters set the context for collective-bargaining negotiations, in terms of the need to secure concessions from the union, and their ability to finance any agreement with trade unions. For example, the 'strong competitors', such as American and Delta, had the financial resources to respond to route and price competition, and were better able to negotiate changes to workrules and wage savings, in return for job security guarantees. 'Weaker' competitors, such as Continental and Eastern, pursued short-term business strategies aimed at achieving financial stability and avoiding insolvency. These carriers were generally able to negotiate wage reductions and costs savings but not changes to workrules, which unions were reluctant to make permanent.

Kochan *et al.* (1984) make a similar point about the response of US tyre producers to import penetration in the rapidly growing US radial tyre market in the late 1970s. Goodyear, the market leader in sales volume, chose

Table 1.2 *Three levels of industrial relations activity*

Level	Employers	Unions	Government
Long term strategy and policy-making	Business strategies Investment Human resource strategies	Political strategies Representation strategies Organising strategies	Macroeconomics and social policies
Collective bargaining and personnel policy	Personnel policies Negotiation strategies	Collective bargaining strategies	Labour law and administration
Workplace and individual–organisation relationships	Supervisory style Worker participation Job design and work organisation	Contract administration Worker participation Job design and work organisation	Labour standards Worker participation Individual rights

Source: Kochan *et al.* (1986: 17)

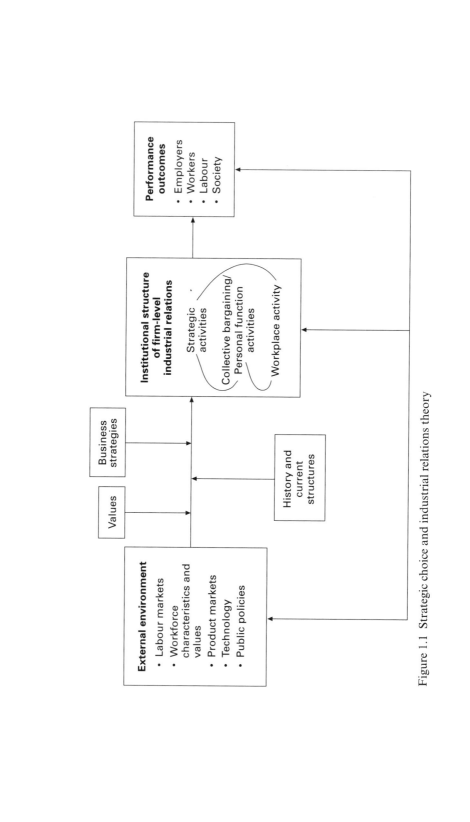

Figure 1.1 Strategic choice and industrial relations theory

to compete on price in every market, and was successful in tying investment in new plant and operations to concessions on workrules (1984: 32). Firestone sought to consolidate its operations and to compete in those markets where it could maintain a high market share. It had the largest reduction in employment, and was the most successful in gaining concessions, partly because it was closing some plants but staying in the tyre business. Goodrich had been diversifying out of the tyre business and was less successful in negotiating concessions, since it had already consolidated much of its operations. Uniroyal faced the worst financial position, and found itself competing in all markets but not in volume and without low-cost modern plants. It closed three of its five plants but was less able to achieve concessions because of pressure to cut its losses.

The central contribution of the strategic choice studies lies in showing how choices over business policy and industrial relations policy structure the response of industry firms to a largely common product market threat; and how these responses in turn may give rise to wide variation in the nature and extent of workrule reform. The primary weakness of these studies is their failure to detail the process by which such choices are arrived at. As Sisson and Marginson (1995: 93) note, the model implies a straightforward process of strategy formulation and implementation. It says little about the degree of choice available to management, nor about how choice is shaped by the interest groups, such as trade unions, with which management interacts. Edwards (1995) observes that the strategic choice model 'does little more than list the parties to industrial relations and their interactions' and, that it is a representation of choice-making with 'much of the politics removed' (1995: 93).

Other studies have been criticised for under-playing the degree of discretion which may be available to management in formulating industrial relations policy. Storey and Sisson (1993), for example, criticise the 'Harvard' model of HRM (Beer *et al.* 1984), with its stress upon responding to the interests of organisational 'stakeholders', and for its advocacy of 'one preferred and superior set of HR policy choices' (1993: 53). Others have argued that industrial relations policy is essentially contingent upon business policy and the external economic context. Schuler and Jackson (1987), for example, derive a set of human resource policies which are consistent with Porter's (1980) competitive strategy alternatives of low cost, high quality or differentiation. For instance, a firm competing on the basis of low cost may logically adopt an anti-collective-bargaining stance intended to drive down wages (1987: 209–13). Friedman (1977) argued that the utilisation of the alternative managerial strategies of 'direct control' or 'responsible autonomy' may be conditional upon external market conditions. For example, 'responsible autonomy', which implies a relaxation of close labour supervision and, possibly increased job satisfaction, may be more appropriate in a tight labour market where management affords a high priority to labour retention. Storey and Sisson (1993) criticise such contingency models for their rational planning assumptions, in that management is implicitly attributed with the power and information sufficient to align its human resource policies with the external environment. Such a view neglects the complexities and uncertainties of managerial strategic choice.

Other studies have gone further by analysing the degree to which markets limit the choice available to management. Marchington and Parker (1990) conducted case studies of four firms in different industry sectors. They show how the room for manoeuvre in management policy is framed by product market 'power', which comprises the degree of competitive pressure from other producers, such as barriers to entry, and the extent of pressure from consumers, such as the level and stability of consumer demand. For example, the chemical company's more orderly product market permitted a developmental approach to employee relations (1990: 248), while the engineering company's more turbulent environment was linked to its confrontational management style. Similarly, Pauuwe (1991) distinguishes between management's 'adaptive' behaviour, which is determined by the competitive context, and 'idiosyncratic' behaviour, which is more discretionary. He maintains that the leeway for idiosyncratic behaviour will increase as firms trade in monopolistic, rather than highly competitive markets, as firms pursue quality rather than low-cost competitive strategies, as the ratio of labour costs to total cost (LC/TC) decreases, and as financial resources increase. These studies usefully analyse the extent to which economic pressures may constrain managerial choice but they give less attention to how any available discretion is actually exercised.

Studies of public enterprises have shown that the political environment may be thought of as emitting a sequence of ambiguous signals which are interpreted by management. The Post Office, for example, was set 'multiple and incommensurate' goals by the array of state bodies responsible for its regulation (Batstone, Ferner and Terry 1984). For example, telecommunications management had to reconcile demands for long-term investment in a digital infrastructure, with short-term needs to maintain and update the existing system. In the light of these disparate obligations, the corporation enjoyed some latitude in formulating its strategy of greater 'commercialism', in the extent to which it conformed to cost and revenue targets and pricing guidelines, and in reconciling its twin objectives of operating efficiency and labour consent.

Ferner's (1988) comparative study of British Rail and the Spanish state-owned railway, RENFE, shows that in neither case was the state able simply to impose its demands for more commercial efficiency upon the enterprises in question. Rather, the states' interpretation of 'commercialism' was itself variable and rapidly shifting. The state was able to shape the environment of the public corporations, by changing the costs and benefits to management of pursuing different policies (1988: 154). The enterprises had to be attuned to the need for politically symbolic action but in so doing, they could deploy their power resources to adjust their industrial relations priorities in terms of co-operation or conflict with trade unions.

Management's role in mediating and translating economic pressures into specific courses of action also has application in private-sector organisations. Child and Smith (1987) distinguish the 'objective' conditions of firms' environment, such as the degree of product market concentration or the height of entry barriers, from the 'cognitive arena', senior managers' constructs of the market environment and its operating dynamics (1987: 566). Smith, Child and Rowlinson (1990) show that choice-making at Cadbury was an essentially political process, in which several strategic visions were held by those in power, with the advocates of these positions competing to determine the strategic outcome. The adopted policy reflected a distinct set of corporate relationships, which included a company history of Quakerism and a 'benevolent' approach to employee welfare. Management style became more aggressive following the merger with Schweppes. 'Contextual economic pressures' were clearly relevant, but these were 'attenuated and mediated by cultural and social factors peculiar to the history and life of the particular organisation' (1990: 98).

These studies point to an 'interpretative' view of strategy as a 'pattern in a stream of decisions' (Mintzberg 1978, quoted in Storey and Sisson 1993: 69). This perspective conceives strategy as a social process, which emerges from decisions taken at several levels of the organisation. These decisions are shaped by individual managers' frames of reference, by the culture and norms of the organisation and by its organisation structure. Such a position may aid considerably our understanding of how economic crisis may give rise to a diversity of change management policies within any single industry sector, and is considered at greater length in the following section.

Strategic choice under crisis conditions

Commentators in a range of disciplines have portrayed economic crisis as a triggering event, in that the shift in market conditions is of such a magnitude that it necessitates remedial action in the form of organisational change. Evolutionary economics, for example, assumes that ingrained routines are dislodged, and that the search for more efficient practices is set in train, by external events such as intense competitive pressures or a shift in available production technology (Aldrich 1979, Nelson and Winter 1982). In strategic management, writers have conceived of 'action thresholds, where stimuli accumulate to the point where they must be recognised by management (Mintzberg, Raisinghani and Theoret 1976), or 'perceived imbalances', where the cost of inaction increases to the point where it can no longer be tolerated by management (Dutton and Duncan 1987: 282).

An additional quality of economic crisis is that it increases uncertainty. One of the defining characteristics of a crisis is the rupturing of precedent; the conditions which pertain in a crisis are qualitatively different to those which preceded it. In addition, events may change rapidly, as was the case with the economy moving quickly into recession in the early 1980s in Britain. The effect may be that crisis conditions create a strong imperative for management to implement reforms, such as measures to reduce operating costs, in order to secure the immediate survival of the firm. But such decisions must be taken in a context in which the available information signals are ambiguous and contradictory, and must be discerned amid a backdrop of irrelevant 'noise' and other interference (Hodgson 1988). In short, management may be faced with a situation in which it is required rapidly to solve complex and ill-defined problems, what Mason and Mitroff (1981) term 'wicked' problems, on the basis of partial and questionable information about its environment.

In addition to raising levels of uncertainty and complexity, economic crisis has a further effect in that it disturbs established procedures for problem formulation and solution. Since one of the defining conditions of a crisis is the absence of precedent, the problems which it occasions may be highly irregular, if not unique. Consequently, there may be no established framework – 'no proven algorithm', as Lyles and Thomas (1988: 132) put it – for defining and analysing such issues. As such, the method management employ to diagnose and formulate a problem may be critical to the outcome that is reached.

Much will depend upon managerial 'frames of reference' – the accumulation of beliefs, assumptions and presumed cause and effect relationships – which are brought to bear upon an issue. This is what psychologists term 'cognitive schema', a 'general term for the knowledge structure or set of expectations that an individual draws upon to guide interpretation, inference and action in any particular situation' (Boland *et al.* 1990: 197). Individuals' belief structures are in part subconscious, and perceivers may not be fully aware of how their preferences and orientations inform their reading of a problem situation. Groups of senior managers may also evolve frames of reference which are similar in certain respects. Prahalad and Bettis (1986) for example, speak of a 'dominant managerial logic', whereby interaction leads members to develop features of their schemata that they share. Others have spoken of 'shared understandings' among elite managers which 'filter' the perceived realities facing the firm (Donaldson and Lorsch 1983: 79).

Cognitive schema may vary widely, even among managers competing in a single industry segment. Reger (1990), for example, found that Chicago bankers had a 'surprisingly low level of agreement' over the main strategic dimensions of their industry, such as the implications of deregulation. Such variation may in part be attributable to differences in the background of individual managers, such as their education and functional expertise. Underlying personality traits may shape decision-making styles, as may factors such as individual managers' ability to sort and code information, and their tolerance of risk (Haley and Stumpf 1989, Wally and Baum 1994).

Given the high level of uncertainty in crisis situations, managers may be prone to accept more readily information signals that are consistent with their cognitive schema, and, even subconsciously, to discount or ignore data that contradict their underlying belief systems. Such information may be disregarded for several reasons (Kieseler and Sproull 1982, Beyer *et al.* 1997). First, the quantity and/or quality of data may be such that it fails to reach a threshold level of significance. Secondly, alternative streams of data may be deemed more relevant or more reliable. Thirdly, the available information may not fall into any pre-existing categories, so that it is not subject to analysis. Managers' judgment of the likelihood of an event may also be biased towards events that are easily recalled by the memory, such as those that occurred recently, or those which are associated with intense emotions (Schwenk 1988: 43).

Managers are also constrained in their ability to absorb and process information. Behavioural economists have long accepted the notion of 'bounded rationality', that rational actors are significantly constrained by limitations of information and calculation (Cyert and March 1992: 214). Such considerations may be especially apt in the context of a crisis, where the time-span for decision-making may be unusually short. To cope with information overload, managers may draw upon heuristics – rules of thumb – which simplify and accelerate the process of decision-making. This may introduce a further bias into choice, by limiting the scope of search for alternatives, or by skewing the process towards one outcome above others.

The scope for action that managers perceive may also frame the decision which is eventually reached. The degree to which a problem is considered solvable depends in part upon available resources, and in part upon managerial knowledge of the barriers that it faces (Dutton and Duncan 1988). Weick (1979) has argued that managers are much more ignorant than is commonly realised about the constraints in their environment. Managers, he maintains, collude to avoid tests which may lead to learning because such tests may be associated with anticipations of pain or other negative emotions.

Cognition is also shaped by the prevailing institutional and organisational structure, which may determine flows of information, or influence goals, such as the importance of short-term profitability. Wally and Baum's

(1994) survey of 151 US CEOs found that decision speed was faster in more centralised organisations and slower in establishments with more formalised procedures. 'Political' factors, such as control over resources, or the degree of normative consensus among senior managers, may also condition decision-making outcomes (Schwenk 1989). Amason (1996), for example, argues that decision quality may be worsened by 'affective' conflict such as personal hostility between managers, but improved by 'cognitive' conflict, or disagreement over ideas. The underlying notion is that exposure to a wider pool of ideas may encourage the adoption of a more efficient solution.

In summary, crisis situations are denoted by the profusion of information cues, which must be interpreted and deciphered by management against a backdrop of high uncertainty. Managers' perception of such signals is conditioned by their system of beliefs and preferences, which they may be only partially aware of. These cognitive schemas may be deeply embedded within the personality make-up of individuals, so that managers may become 'trapped' in a set way of framing an issue (Boland *et al*. 1990: 219). The information-processing capacity of managers is also bounded, and is shaped by political and resource considerations, and by the administrative system within which a decision is taken. Consequently, firms may differ in their estimation of the perceived urgency of a crisis and in the perceived feasibility of finding a solution (Dutton and Duncan 1987). The outcome may be a spectrum of responses to a competitive crisis from firms within any single industry sector, of the sort detailed in the strategic choice studies above. These may range from (i) avoidance of the situation, based upon selective perception of the environment and a bias towards the *status quo*; (ii) adaptation, characterised by incremental change and a preference for 'satisfycing', or taking action sufficient to offset the immediate crisis; and (iii) 'decisive' change, where the stress is upon action generation and achieving momentum (e.g., Lyles and Thomas 1988).

Discussion

This first chapter has shown that there exists a great deal of data about how the economic and social structure changed in Britain in the 1980s, and also, through large scale surveys, of the formal, institutional contours of industrial relations. It has been argued that economic pressures and employment law reforms may have stimulated work restructuring, which may have some validity at the aggregate level of the economy. But it is also necessary to account for the differences in the context and processes of reform, which may be critical to the broad pattern of change. The strategic choice studies in the US have shown that a competitive crisis may lead to a wide variation in the nature and extent of workrule change among companies within a common industry group. In Britain, numerous studies have demonstrated a trend away from Donovan orthodoxy in the management of employment relations, towards a wider variety of systems and styles. The central question is how to account for this greater plurality. We have seen that the strategic choice studies fail to address the politics and the uncertainties of managerial decision-making. Other studies have suggested that the economic environment may give off a series of equivocal signals which must be interpreted by managers, and that such perceptions may be structured by a variety of cognitive, organisational, political and institutional factors, which may differ according to the individual and the firm or establishment under consideration.

In the present study, we will show that most panel firms experienced a severe economic crisis in the early 1980s. This took the form of a collapse in corporate profits, reinforced by capital market pressures, such as the threat of a stock market takeover, or by enforced changes of ownership, such as privatisation. These changes were associated with the reform of management policy, and a shift away from collective-bargaining-centred policies, together with a decline in management support for union organisation. Managers also reported an increase in their perceived bargaining power. Union security, judged by the level of union density, the presence of collective bargaining and by the informal closed shop, remained largely intact for manual and craft workers, but was much more prone to erosion for white-collar workers, among whom the ethic of union organisation may have been less well entrenched. Widespread changes to substantive work-rules were reported, but the extent of change varied widely, from firms that registered few, if any, major reforms to working practices, to those that had engaged in a major restructuring. Hence, the pattern that emerges is one of fine-grained changes to the system of procedural and substantive work-rules, the degree and nature of which differ between industry sectors, occupational groups and between individual firms and establishments. This variation is analysed in terms of the 'refraction' of competitive shocks through widely differing interpretative frameworks, which created a diverse array of industrial relations policies and varying trajectories of workrule reform. Firms differed in the degree to which the crisis situation was translated into an ongoing momentum for change, in the extent to which change was routed through collective-bargaining procedures or to which procedures were bypassed or even dismantled, and in the degree to which firms were risk-bearing or risk-averse in attempting to secure reforms.

There are a further seven chapters to the book, which deal with data and collective bargaining (chapter 2); union security (chapter 3); work organisation (chapter 4); employers' associations (chapter 5); competitive pressures (chapter 6); management policy (chapter 7); and a discussion (chapter 8).

2   Data and collective bargaining

Chapter 1 set out the main themes of the study and outlined the data only in brief. This chapter describes the data in greater detail, and goes on to consider two points of central importance – the coverage of collective bargaining and the level of pay determination. As noted earlier, data derive from an interview survey of fifty predominantly highly unionised British companies. Data are longitudinal in scope: they were collected at two points in time – 1979 and 1991. Brief reference will also be made to an interview survey of fifteen employers' associations, also in the unionised sectors of the economy. Together, these data address the three analytical themes set out in chapter 1. The first theme is the nature of environmental pressure, and the extent to which the management response was characterised by strategic choice. The second theme is how this process fashioned the pattern of management industrial relations policy, and the extent to which management departed from a policy of joint regulation. The third theme is the combined impact of economic crisis and management policy shifts upon the institutional characteristics and actors' conduct at the workplace.

For companies, the respondents were mainly senior personnel managers, interviewed individually or in pairs. All interviews were conducted jointly by Stephen Dunn of the London School of Economics and the present writer. The basis of comparison is data collected as part of the LSE/Department of Employment Closed Shop Project (Dunn and Gennard 1984). This survey examined the extent of the closed shop in British industry in 1979. Team members interviewed 100 firms and twenty employers' associations. They collected data extending considerably beyond the closed shop, to encompass the characteristics of markets, internal organisation, management policy and unionisation.

A subset of firms in 1991 was selected for re-interviewing. The basis of selection was entirely non-random. By definition, the study excludes firms which had ceased to exist in the intervening period. Small groups of firms were chosen in the main industrial sectors studied in 1979. These included engineering, car manufacturing, brewing, publishing, retailing and textiles. Of the fifty-three or fifty-four firms approached, almost all agreed to co-operate. Only four rejections were received, technically a response rate of over 95 per cent. One reason for this high rate is that companies were made strongly aware that they had previously co-operated with the project, in 1979, and that results had been treated confidentially.

The level of analysis in this study is the bargaining unit, or group of workers. For example, company number 12, a vehicle manufacturer, contained a number of bargaining groups in 1979, including production operatives, various craft groups, the transport and delivery section and non-manual staff. These groups then formed the starting point of the 1991 interviews. Comparison, in certain cases, was impeded because the 1979 reports were directed at the closed shop, and frequently disregarded those groups where it was quickly ascertained that no closed shop was present. For example, in firms numbered 19 and 26, the largest unit in 1979 was a non-manual group with low union density. The researchers paid scant attention to these groups. In these cases, the focus is upon the largest group for which detailed information is available, which are primarily manual groups.

In certain cases, the largest group of employees had been merged or amalgamated with another group during the course of the study. In two cases, in 1979 there was multi-employer but no employer-level bargaining. By 1991, multi-employer bargaining had been discontinued and all agreements were at employer level. In these two companies, in 1979 and 1991, the same employees are covered, although in 1979 these employees were subsumed within a much larger bargaining unit.

Interviewees were primarily located at UK corporate headquarters. A distinction is drawn between corporate, subsidiary and establishment levels, and confined to the British management hierarchy. Head offices located abroad were excluded. Overall, almost all the respondents were at British corporate headquarters. In 1979, forty-nine of the fifty respondents were at this level, with one at subsidiary. In 1991, forty-seven were at corporate headquarters, and three at subsidiary. However, in a number of cases, the corporate 'headquarters' was also the main factory or production site and the distinction between the three levels ought not to be exaggerated.

It is not easy to classify accurately organisations that operate in a number of different manufacturing and service sectors. The most common technique employed is classification by primary sector of activity, where employment or revenue generated is greatest. Primary sector of employment has been adopted here. Because firms are clustered into highly unionised manufacturing and process industries, the Standard Industrial Classification has been revised from ten divisions to six. Division 4, into which many firms were classed, has been subdivided. A number of the thinly populated divisions have been amalgamated and some omitted

Table 2.1 *Comparability of firms 1979–1991*

Number	Standard Industrial Classification division	Industry	1979 (n = 50)	1991 (n = 50)	Change
1	1, 2	Energy, water, materials, minerals, chemicals	8	8	–
2	3	Vehicle manufacture, electrical and mechanical engineering	13	12	–1
3	4100, 4200	Food manufacture, brewing, tobacco	7	7	–
4	4300, 4700, 4800	Rubber, textiles, plastics, print, paper, publishing	8	9	+1
5	5, 7	Construction, transport, communications	7	7	–
6	6/9700	Distribution: retail, wholesale, film	7	7	–

Note:
Classification based on a modified version of the Standard Industrial Classification division

entirely. Between seven and thirteen firms fall into each revised division. This scale reveals the clustering of panel firms into a small number of industry sectors (Table 2.1). The panel is not at all representative of the broad population of British firms.

Table 2.1 also shows the comparability of data across time. It is important to ensure that like firms in 1979 and 1991 are being compared. Comparative assessment may be impeded by high rates of attrition, as firms suffer bankruptcy, are taken over by competitors, are privatised and so on. The first measure is the industry in which the firm trades, classed according to the primary sector of employment. On this measure, only one of the fifty firms falls into a different industry sector in 1991, relative to 1979. Almost all firms continued to operate in the same industry sector during the period of study. A second measure of comparability is the name of the firm. This may change due to takeovers, amalgamations or privatisation. Five of the fifty firms had altered in this way; three had been amalgamated and two had been privatised. These five firms were not concentrated in any single industry sector but were dispersed across a range of sectors. A final issue is comparability of bargaining units and in each case the identical unit – or group of workers – has been compared in the two time periods.

This analysis suggests that the study is comparing like bargaining units and, in the large majority of instances, like firms over time. Based upon

Table 2.2 *Employment in firms 1979–1991*

Class	Number of employees	Number of firms 1979 (n = 47)	Number of firms 1991 (n = 47)
1	1,000–4,999	4	9
2	5,000–9,999	7	7
3	10,000–24,999	12	13
4	25,000–49,999	11	10
5	50,000–100,000	8	6
6	100,001+	5	2

Notes:
1. n = 47; for three firms a comparison of size could not be made.
2. In both periods mean firm size falls into class 3.

primary sector of employment, panel firms have remained in much the same industries between 1979 and 1991. Two factors have given rise to this consistency. Data were collected in 1979 at the level of the bargaining unit. Even where the firm has ceased to exist as a corporate entity, it is still usually possible to isolate the same group of workers and their successors within the new body. Stability in the main area of operation has occurred because the firms are large and placed into broad classes. General distinctions may obscure important shifts in activity such as the penetration of new markets or the development of fresh products.

A second issue is the size of panel firms, defined as the total number of full-time employees employed in Britain. The 1979 report provides a breakdown of total employment by each plant, and comparisons can easily be made, even when the firm has changed its structure or been amalgamated with other firms. Size is classified on a scale that gives six divisions based on number of full-time employees. Data are presented at Table 2.2.

There has been a fall in the number of firms in each of the largest three classes of employment, those above 25,000 employees, and a doubling of firms in the smallest class, 1,000 to 4,999 employees. The table disguises the full extent of change. Of the forty-seven firms for which a comparison could be made, only eleven remained in the same band of employment and only seven increased in size. These seven firms were concentrated in divisions 5 (construction, transport and communication) and division 6 (distribution). The reasons advanced for this reduction in size are those frequently mentioned, such as the closure of non-viable plants and the concentration of production at the most efficient sites.

It is worth commenting that firms in this panel are relatively large, compared, for example, with Marginson *et al.*'s study (1988). Over half of

Marginson's firms employed fewer than 10,000 employees but in this study in 1991 only one-third of firms did so (1988: 23). The trend for employment in manufacturing and process firms to fall while those in services, such as communications and retail distribution, expands is confirmed in other sources. Average company employment in Edwards' sample of manufacturing firms fell from 31,500 to 24,600 between 1978 and 1984 (1987: 26).

Interview data were supplemented by references to panel companies in *Industrial Relations Review and Report* and in Financial Times *Profile*. The *Industrial Relations Review and Report* is published fortnightly, and includes reports of strikes, annual settlements, productivity deals and working practices. Most of the firms in the panel featured regularly in this press. All references to panel firms in the *Industrial Relations Review and Report* between 1979 and 1991 were recorded. FT *Profile* is a database containing reports of companies featured in the Financial Times. The two sources combined were used to amass supplementary data about issues mentioned in interview, such as further details about a strike, or exact levels of published profits and losses in any one year. We also draw upon examples of collective agreements, which include data about union recognition, disputes procedures, pay levels and work practices, which were collected as part of the study.

Data on employers' associations follow much the same format as those for companies. These data are also longitudinal in scope, covering the period from 1979 to 1990, with interviews conducted by the same researchers. Respondents were usually the senior industrial relations officer or executive responsible. Employers' associations were also selected for interview on a non-random basis. We wrote to the twenty associations interviewed as part of the 1979 study; eighteen of these agreed to take part. Three of the associations interviewed have been excluded from the results because field notes were unreliable or these interviews covered a rather different range of issues. Additional data were also collected from *Industrial Relations Review and Report* and from multi-employer collective agreements. The 1979 Closed Shop survey included a detailed report on each association.

The panel of employers' associations covers much the same unionised manufacturing and processing sectors as the companies. The adjusted Standard Industrial Classification, which was used above, is again used here. Results are presented in Table 2.3. At least one association was interviewed in each industry sector. The distribution in Table 2.3 reflects the small number of encompassing associations in sectors, such as heavy engineering, together with a much larger number of associations in sectors such as rubber, textiles, print, publishing and paper. In a small number of sectors, such as energy and water, the relevant association declined to co-operate, and the study does not refer to this area.

Table 2.3 *Classification of employers' associations*

Number	Standard Industrial Classification division	Industry	Number (= 15)
1	1, 2	Energy, water, materials, minerals, chemicals	1
2	3	Vehicle manufacturing, electrical and mechanical engineering	2
3	4100, 4200	Food manufacture, brewing, tobacco	1
4	4300, 4700, 4800	Rubber, textiles, plastics, print, paper, publishing	9
5	5, 7	Construction, transport, communications	1
6	6/9700	Distribution (retail, wholesale, film)	1

Note:
Classification based on modified version of the Standard Industrial Classification

Contribution of the data

Specific research issues were highlighted in chapter 1. There has recently been a lively debate about the use of research methods in industrial relations (McCarthy 1994, Millward and Hawes 1995, Fernie and Woodland 1995), and it is important to locate the present study within these debates. The themes addressed in the introduction are fundamentally those of social action and process, and the extent to which each were demonstrated within the union sector. These issues include how management interpreted change in the economic and social structure. They refer to the dynamics of management policy formation under crisis conditions, and the degree to which management consciously and deliberately exercised choice. Finally, research themes concern the conditioning effect of environmental change upon the complex of workrules and administrative structures at the workplace.

These themes required semi-structured interviews, where the views and opinions of respondents could be probed at length. In interview, our intention was to create an informal atmosphere, one that encouraged the interviewees to reflect, talk openly and in confidence. Requests were usually made for an interview lasting for ninety minutes but the majority continued for longer, some considerably so. If there was a common pattern to the interviews, it was that subjects were initially guarded in their comments and stuck firmly to a rather sanitised version of events but as the conversation progressed they would talk more freely and candidly.

The distinctive feature of this study is the combined attention to broad patterns and specific processes. The study explores the rate of change in key institutional arrangements, such as the coverage of collective bargaining. This material may then be supplemented by material on process. Interviewees were probed for their reasons about why collective bargaining had or had not been retained, how this links with other variables such as union density or the closed shop, and in what ways external conditions had affected these developments.

As such, this study ought to be seen as complementary both to the main surveys and to intensive case studies. Large-scale surveys cover a far greater number of establishments and organisations than has been possible here. Because they typically employ structured samples, they are also able to claim their findings are generalisable to the broader population. No such claims are made for the present study. But because large-scale question-naires typically utilise a pre-set questionnaire, administered by post or by a professional interviewer, they are less able to shed light on the processes of change. Equally, case studies usually offer a more detailed treatment of process, drawing upon the views of management, trade union officials and employees, which was not possible in this study. But case studies are neces-sarily confined to a small number of organisations, which raises questions about the typicality of their findings. The present study covers a sufficient number of large firms in Britain to offer some broader findings about indus-trial relations in the union sector, even if these findings cannot be general-ised to a larger population. It is also possible to highlight the comments of individual interviewees to address specific processes.

These observations are, of course, confined to the union sector. The composition of the panel of companies was determined by the 1979 study, which investigated the extent of the closed shop in British industry. The study therefore focused upon the manufacturing and processing industries in which the closed shop was likely to be identified, and these traits continue to define the study. These are, however, the sectors in which much industrial relations reform was said to be concentrated in the 1980s. For example, Sisson (1993), reviewing the evidence in WIRS3, found the discernible 'frag-ments' of HRM to be clustered in unionised establishments. CLIRS2 also points to similar findings. In the US, Eaton and Voos (1992) found that workplace restructuring was more common in union companies. Storey *et al.*'s (1994, summarised in Storey 1995: 17–20) questionnaire of 560 employing organisations with fifteen or more employees in Leicestershire found that activity on personnel management and work restructuring was especially a feature of large, unionised organisations. The industries covered in the present study are those in which union representation was most deeply entrenched and in which union job controls and restrictions upon labour productivity were most likely to have been found in 1979. And these sectors are most likely to have been markedly affected by product market crisis in the 1980s, and by changes in legislative provisions on the closed shop and industrial disputes. In short, if a transformation of industrial relations is to be detected anywhere in the British economy, it is most likely to be within this panel of companies.

Plainly, this study examines the perspective of senior management, whose interpretation of events may differ from trade unionists or employees. Our enquiry also asked respondents to comment retrospectively upon events. When recalling actions in which they have been involved, interviewees tend naturally to have selective and rather rosy recall. They may involuntarily suppress incidents that reflect poorly upon their own standing, such as the experiment that turned out badly. Furthermore, causal processes are rarely straightforward to ascribe, even when the analytical framework is clear. Parties may construe an event, and those factors that gave rise to it, in different terms. Processes are often best described in terms of a multiplicity of factors not all of which are known to a single person. If our concentration upon senior management may be justified, it is because these actors were of central importance in determining the industrial relations response to competitive shock. On matters such as the utilisation of employment law, and the formulation of labour management policy, the initiative lay with the tier of senior personnel managers that forms the basis of this study. Even a hugely expanded number of interviews would only achieve a better approximation.

To overcome the problem of the sheer amount of data collected, which it would be tedious and impracticable to relate, the main approach in the study is to summarise the data using short tables and elementary scales of classification. These findings are then elaborated upon through comments and examples. At its most relevant, this discursive material can give some of the feel of change. Although a question prompt was used throughout the study, the issues that were developed and discussed at length varied between interviews. Consequently, in certain cases, the data do not cover the full panel of companies. There are also the inevitable attendant difficulties of imprecision in questions asked or in responses given, misunderstanding and illegible notes. Where this occurs, it has been noted.

One of the central issues raised in the introductory chapter is the coverage of collective bargaining and the level of pay bargaining among panel firms. The chapter now turns to a discussion of these two pivotal issues.

Collective bargaining

Firms are 'covered' by collective bargaining when the primary means of setting pay and conditions of employment for the largest bargaining unit is through negotiation between an employer and recognised unions. Firms

Table 2.4 *Coverage of*
collective bargaining

Year	Number of firms (n = 50)
1979	47
1991	42

Note:
'Coverage' where the primary
method of determining pay and
conditions for the largest
bargaining unit is negotiation
between an employer and trade
unions.

are not covered when pay is set for the largest group of workers by managerial *diktat*, by individual appraisal or by 'spot' contract rates. In both time periods detailed data are available about collective bargaining. The results are summarised in Table 2.4.

Over 90 per cent of panel firms in 1979 were covered by collective bargaining. This is a high figure. But it is not unduly surprising given the size of panel firms and that the panel was originally determined on the probability of firms operating a closed shop. The three firms not bargaining in 1979 were all in division 6 (retail distribution). Of the forty-seven firms bargaining in 1979, five had discontinued by 1991. Three of these five firms were in division 5 (construction, transport and communications). There have been no examples of discontinuation in division 1, energy, minerals and chemicals, nor in division 3 (food, tobacco and brewing).

Some hesitant contrasts may be drawn with other studies. The Warwick survey asked in manufacturing whether unions were 'recognised by management for negotiating pay and conditions'. They found that a union was recognised for manual workers in three-quarters of workplaces and for non-manual workers in just over one-third of workplaces (Brown 1981: 53). These figures are consistent with those in this study.

WIRS3 also enquired about recognition for negotiating terms and conditions. The survey found a 'substantial decline in the extent of recognition since 1984' (Millward *et al.* 1992: 70). In private manufacturing this shrinkage was especially a feature of the vehicles, engineering and print sectors. These two movements are consistent with the present study. But WIRS notes that the decline of bargaining was clustered principally among new firms and also among smaller firms: 'In establishments with fewer than 200 employees the fall [in recognition] was substantial; above this size there was hardly any change' (1992: 72). These findings may also be easily reconciled with the present study, where the vast majority of firms had retained collective bargaining for the largest bargaining group. We shall take up a number of these themes in the following chapter, which examines derecognition.

Cases on collective bargaining

Some of the reasons expressed by managers for the maintenance or termination of collective bargaining may now be probed. A first point is why joint determination continues to be the primary means of setting pay and conditions for almost 90 per cent of panel firms. This issue is more puzzling than it might initially appear. Neo-classical economists have stylised unions as monopoly sellers of labour with the capacity to drive up the relative pay of their members. This, it is claimed, has a negative effect upon employers' financial performance. A number of economists have posited an inverse association between union presence, especially the pre-entry closed shop, and performance criteria such as pay, productivity, jobs and profits, which is consistent with the 'monopoly seller' assumption (Metcalf 1993).

From this view, employers would prefer to derecognise trade unions in order to offset negative efficiency effects and to gain a comparative advantage over their competitors. Yet the overwhelming majority of firms have not done so. The following cases illustrate three reasons why. The first is F32, in division 4 (rubber, textiles, printing etc.), which has not attempted to end collective bargaining because it fears organisation by a more aggressive union:

The fear is that the industry would become like the car industry. Many colleagues are still frightened of unions although this is getting less. They want to be working with the reps of labour, not against them and the present industry unions want the industry to succeed.

The industry unions are not militant. They have a clear interest in the survival of the sector. Union recognition has been retained because the alternative, de-unionisation, brings with it the threat of a more assertive union and the perceived risk of less favourable performance.

This is not the case made most frequently for continued persistence with collective bargaining. Most panel firms do not recognise a single industry union but a variety of craft, manual and non-manual unions. For these firms two justifications are expressed. The first reason is the limited relevance of collective bargaining to economic performance. For example, F12 is in division 2 (vehicles, shipbuilding and engineering). A senior manager stated:

there are few areas where we disagree with unions. There is very little which we couldn't go to the unions for. So we don't wage war and we are not anti-union. If you've got unions you might as well have sensible agreements with them. They are not the problem. Most of the main difficulties revolve around management.

On this view collective bargaining is not a significant barrier to the improvement of firm performance. Other factors are more important. There is little incentive to attack an institution that is thought not to produce negative outcomes.

Less often declared than the 'irrelevance' argument but present in a sizeable subset of firms is the view that collective bargaining is a positive source of value-added. F17 is a traditional manufacturing firm in division 4, rubber, textiles, printing etc. It recognises a number of manual, craft and non-manual unions. The personnel director claimed that:

we accepted that our procedural relationships were good and that we had a substantive problem. The unions understood that we were just not competitive. Procedure was respected. We harnessed the union's support. Change was accepted and done in a sensible and humane way. We have never had problems with the union over improving standards.

Collective bargaining procedures proved to be a useful conduit for the implementation of change. Bargaining contributed to the improvement of performance because it provided a framework within which alterations could be made. It would have been perverse and destructive to dismantle joint institutions.

Collective bargaining had in some cases been retained through fear of organisation by other, more assertive unions. More often, bargaining institutions were thought either to be of limited relevance to performance outcomes, or positively to enhance them. Rarely did managers offer the opinion that the products of union recognition were unwarranted wage rates or constraints on efficiency. It may be that these responses display a degree of 'cognitive dissonance'. Interviewees may have been attempting to justify adherence to an inferior system because they lacked the power to dispense with it. If so, few signals were received from interviewees of a latent hostility to collective bargaining, although this possibility cannot be discounted.

Some instructive examples may also be given about those firms in which bargaining had not been continued. The only firms not bargaining in 1979 were those in the retail distribution sector, traditionally an area of low union organisation. Of the five firms no longer covered in 1991, a twofold distinction may be made. Two firms in sector 5 (construction, transport and communications) had not discontinued bargaining. Rather, bargaining just covered a minority of employees. Management contracting had become the dominant mode of work organisation, with each site responsible for cost and delivery. Sites increasingly disregarded the working rate stipulated in industry working rules and hired labour on individual contracts and market-related pay. 'Spot' rates of pay extended across the workforce and displaced nationally negotiated rates.

Collective bargaining had been deliberately terminated at three firms. Each of these firms operates in a different industry sector. Each had in common the intention to end union recognition as part of a broader over-haul of employment practices. F8 falls in sector 5 (construction, transport and communications).

A number of factors came together really. In 1984 there was pressure on pay rates. We were linked to a broader pay structure, which limited our ability to raise wages and recruit high-calibre graduates. In 1987 the corporate structure of the firm was reorganised. Management responsibility was devolved to independent business units. Personnel was left as a strategic policy-making/guidance division. Our fastest growing subsidiary had chosen not to recognise unions. We thought that derecognition would sit more comfortably with our business policy and would allow us to introduce a performance-related, market-driven system of pay.

The objective here is not the removal of collective bargaining *per se*. Rather bargaining has been ended to expedite the implementation of a fresh personnel strategy, in this case one founded upon individual contracts and performance-based appraisal. This would be a model example of management deliberately sweeping away joint regulation and pushing the individual employment contract to the fore of the employment relationship. But it is characteristic of only a small minority of examples.

Pay determination

Much importance has been accorded to the devolution of pay bargaining. Decentralised pay setting, it is claimed, has freed managers from corporate or industry-wide industrial relations institutions. It has enabled local managers to circumvent joint regulation and introduce individual pay schemes. Successive Conservative administrations in the 1980s strongly encouraged firms to move to locally determined pay and to make wage rates more sensitive to regional market circumstances. Much evidence suggests that pay bargaining has been considerably devolved (Brown and Walsh 1991).

This section explores what happened to pay determination in panel firms. Pay bargaining is an important issue but one which is difficult to study accurately. The standard method of examining the 'most important level at which local pay was fixed' was followed (Brown 1981: 6, Millward *et al.* 1992: 218). This is probably the most feasible approach but it is not without difficulties. One difficulty concerns what is meant by 'important'. The level of pay setting is nebulous at best. Settlements may be formally agreed at one level but strongly influenced by negotiations at another. A number of firms

Table 2.5 *Level of pay determination 1979–1991*

Level	1979 (n = 49)	1991 (n = 49)
Collective bargaining		
Multi-employer	9	0
Corporate	23	10
Subsidiary	2	7
Establishment	12	24
Not collective bargaining		
All-level	3	8
Total	49	49

Note:
n = 49; in one case, response unusable.

said that the rate of pay increase was fixed at the establishment but drew heavily upon the figure agreed at multi-employer level. Classifications have again been made according to the largest bargaining unit in each firm. This method may overlook small but strategically important groups of workers such as craft operatives. It was not possible to distinguish reliably between manual and non-manual occupational groups.

Four levels of bargaining have been separated: multi-employer, corporate, subsidiary and establishment. The respective levels cannot always be clearly made out in practice. Findings are displayed at Table 2.5. A substantial shift is observable away from multi-employer and corporate-level bargaining. Around 20 per cent of the panel named the multi-employer level as the most important in 1979; none did so in 1991. 'Corporate' was the most frequently cited level of bargaining in 1979. In 1991, it was 'establishment'. This is a picture of the wide-spread decentralisation of bargaining to establishment level.

Examining pay determination where pay was not set by collective bargaining may bring out an additional point. Three firms did not bargain in 1979, all in the retail distribution sector. These three firms all set pay in 1979 at the corporate or divisional level, and all continued to do so in 1991. Contrast this with the five firms that discontinued pay bargaining. Of these firms in 1979 three had 'multi-employer' as the most important level while two had 'corporate'. By 1991 each cited 'establishment' as the most important level. This move reinforces the evidence suggesting that union recognition had been terminated as part of a more embracing overhaul of the payment system and employment policy generally.

Looking at the data by industry sector reveals a useful point. Multi-employer bargaining was relatively important in 1979 in division 4 (printing, paper and communications) and in division 5 (transport and communication). This is broadly in line with the findings on multi-employer bargaining in Brown (1981: 10). There is also a sectoral trend to the decentralisation of pay. Devolution of pay bargaining was substantial and widespread in all divisions except division 2 (vehicles and heavy engineering). Here, there was no pronounced movement away from corporate-level pay setting, nor was there a shift to establishment level. Indeed there was in this sector a rare example of the centralisation of pay from the establishment to the corporate centre. Division 2 is anomalous in this respect.

One final issue is whether there were any corporate controls on pay setting at the divisional level or below. A rudimentary taxonomy of guidelines enforced by head offices has been constructed. A distinction may be made between:

1. 'no guide', where lower-level units are able to set internal pay levels independent of external influence;
2. 'advice/approval', where the corporate centre does not explicitly demand adherence to a company rate but may informally attempt to exercise influence; and
3. 'formal limit', where lower-level units are obliged to set pay within a range or based on criteria determined at the corporate centre.

The thirty-two units in 1991 that bargained at the divisional level or below have been examined. Of these, twenty-five had some form of corporate control over pay setting. Data are summarised in Table 2.6. Control most commonly took the form of the imposition of an absolute limit, followed by informal controls such as advice or approval. Less than one-quarter of firms with decentralised bargaining placed 'no guide' on the rate of pay that lower-level units could agree. Industry sectors use controls over pay to differing degrees. In divisions 1 and 5, most firms do have formal controls. Division 2 is exceptional again. Firms here were least likely to devolve bargaining; they were also least likely to impose formal controls where they have done so.

Considerable decentralisation of pay bargaining has been found. About two-thirds of panel firms in 1979 conducted pay bargaining principally at the corporate or multi-employer level; by 1991 about two-thirds bargained at divisional or establishment level. Where bargaining had been entirely discontinued, pay had in each case been devolved to establishment level. Most instances of decentralisation also featured formal or informal control exercised by the centre over pay setting in lower-level units. This trend was consistent across industry sectors with the exception of division 2 (vehicles and heavy engineering). Here firms were less inclined to decentralise and where they had done so less disposed to impose controls over establishment discretion.

The impression of widespread decentralisation of pay determination is

Table 2.6 *Guidelines on pay determined at divisional level or below*

Sector	Industry	1 No guide	2 Advice/ approval	3 Formal limit
1	Energy, water, materials, minerals, chemicals	1	1	4
2	Vehicle manufacture, electrical and mechanical engineering	4	3	1
3	Food manufacture, brewing, tobacco	0	2	3
4	Rubber, textiles, plastics, print, paper, publishing	1	2	3
5	Construction, transport, communications	0	1	3
6	Distribution (retail, wholesale, film)	1	1	1
Total		7	10	15

Note:
n = 32 firms for which the most important bargaining level in 1991 was divisional or establishment.

attenuated by evidence of the influence retained by corporate headquarters. There is some commonality between these findings and those of Millward *et al.* (1992). Multi-employer bargaining is reported to have declined substantially for both manual and non-manual workers (1992: 218). Non-bargained pay determination at the workplace became much more common (1992: 220). But there appeared to be no corresponding increase in bargaining at the establishment level, even within private manufacturing: 'Rather than lead to more plant-level negotiations, the move away from multi-employer negotiations was accompanied by an increase in negotiating structures at enterprise or company level' (Millward *et al.* 1992: 355, quoted in Brown 1993).

This stands out as a major discrepancy between the two data sets. It is again worth underlining the dangers of comparing the present study with the findings in WIRS. However, the above findings are much more consistent with the findings of other studies. Walsh found widespread occurrence of local management being given freedom to negotiate only within strict financial limits and instances of close consultation between factory management and corporate personnel (1993: 424). CLIRS discovered that in three-quarters of cases where there had been a change in pay determination, it had been towards devolution, and that corporate managers were involved in decentralised pay setting in 65 per cent of cases (Marginson *et al.* 1993: 9; see also Marginson *et al.* 1988: 151).

A more detailed look at how and why pay has been decentralised in panel firms is needed.

Cases on pay determination

The trend most frequently identified, for pay determination to be transferred to establishment level with the corporate centre retaining some control over settlement rates, is examined first. F31 is in division 4 (rubber, textiles, printing etc.). The most important point of pay determination in 1979 was multi-employer. 'Strong and ordered' industry bargaining arrangements were adhered to. In 1980, the firm resolved to make the individual business units 'stand alone' and allow managing directors to 'run and take responsibility'. Membership of multi-employer associations was terminated and the industrial relations staff relocated. High-level contacts with trade unions were severed and pay devolved to individual businesses:

Central limits are set on wages. Local managers cannot arbitrarily exceed them. We try to collect data on added value, per cent wage cost and sales/employee. This ensures we know that pay is backed by productivity improvements such as reduced manning or flexibility. This year [1991] it is exceptional for us to allow anything other than pay cuts or freezes.

This combination of decentralisation and limits on the autonomy of subsidiaries was widely observed. It is consonant with the reasons for decentralisation identified by Marginson *et al.* (1993: 8) and Walsh (1993: 413).

In only seven of the thirty-two cases of decentralised bargaining in 1991 was the centre wholly uninterested in subsidiary pay activity. Four of these cases fell within division 2 (vehicles and heavy engineering). F3 trades in this sector. It is an instructive case. The staff headquarters of F3 consists of about forty people, mostly accountants, who control finance through a three-year corporate plan. They do not interfere with the operational decisions of business units. Personnel managers from the various subsidiaries have a monthly liaison and co-ordination meeting where pay is regularly discussed:

questions would be asked if we reported a large increase. We negotiate on a site basis and a large increase could have knock-on effects within the group. Colleagues would get 'miffed' if we couldn't justify an increase as reasonable. There is a little bit of peer pressure but if we thought it right for the business then we could do it.

Even where sites have complete autonomy, sibling businesses may press for some measure of conformity. Informal channels of communication can pressure firms into setting rates commensurate with related businesses.

While the transference of pay bargaining downwards is the most common trend, it is worth recalling that 20 per cent of panel firms in 1991 continued to negotiate over pay at the corporate centre. These firms were found in most divisions although they clustered somewhat in division 2. Some of the reasons for this continued attachment to centralisation may be explored. F21 is in sector 1 (energy, materials and chemicals). It has stable, long-standing collective bargaining institutions. These arrangements arose from a highly centralising agreement of the late 1960s which was intended to check the growth of disputes and incentive payments. This firm has recently been reorganised into a number of independent businesses. Divisions had been abolished but all bargaining over blue- and white-collar terms and conditions continues to be done centrally:

there may be some logic in devolving pay to the businesses and not having company-wide machinery. We tell the businesses that they have total responsibility yet do not let them decide pay. But some sites have more than one business and devolution might result in different pay rates within the same factory. More importantly, at present it is easy to change the composition of the businesses within an overall umbrella of stability.

A centralised bargaining structure is retained because the wider business needs demand labour stability. A strong institutional structure allows potential disruptions to be channelled into procedure and dealt with. A similar rationale was expressed by a number of other firms.

Summary

This chapter has presented a first piece in a more elaborate mosaic of changing industrial relations practices that will be built up in subsequent chapters. Collective bargaining survived largely but not wholly intact. Bargaining institutions continued to be adhered to partly from fear of more aggressive unions. Where firms had withdrawn bargaining rights, they had done so deliberately as part of a generic shift in personnel policy. Also, the main reason expressed for the maintenance of collective bargaining was that joint negotiations were thought either positively to enhance performance or to have no negative effect.

Pay determination has undoubtedly been widely decentralised across panel firms. Yet formal controls continued to operate on the discretion of plant-level managers to set wage rates. This finding implies that a complex process is at work. It suggests the continuation of a degree of formal or informal control over pay bargaining at establishment level. But it does also indicate a widening in the discretion of local managers to set pay rates compared to the previous centralised system.

While these data are of interest in establishing the contours of joint regulation, they say little about the vigour of union organisation. Consequently, chapter 3 assesses union security.

3   Union security

Changes in the extent and form of union security are a central point of enquiry. The joint regulation of the terms and conditions of employment is dependent, at least in part, upon strong trade union organisation. A weakening of union membership and influence may be associated with a shrinkage in the scope of joint regulation and a shift in the frontier of control away from labour. Three of the most accessible indicators of union security are studied in this chapter: union density, derecognition and the closed shop.

Union density

A primary gauge of union presence is density, the proportion of full-time employees who are members of a trade union. Most firms in the panel in both time periods used check-off to deduct union dues directly from members' wages, and the following figures ought to be well informed and based on up-to-date information. The 1979 data breaks down union membership according to plant and occupational class and this degree of detail was useful in making comparisons with 1991. Craft, manual and non-manual occupational classes have been differentiated. Units have been omitted in some cases because the respondent could not give dependable density statistics, because firms did not employ certain categories of labour or because the interview transcripts were unclear or contradictory. Data are displayed in Table 3.1.

Density has fallen in each occupational class. With craft workers the reduction is marginal, for manual workers it is not great. Non-manual density has declined by twelve percentage points. A notable point emerges if we disaggregate these figures by industry sector. Table 3.2 presents these data. In some boxes the number of observations is quite low and caution is advised when interpreting the figures.

With the exception of a small number of craft instances, there has been a decline in density in each industry sector in all occupational classes. This reinforces the picture painted above. One notable point is the general absence of a strong sectoral pattern to decline. Falls in density mostly are

Table 3.1 *Union density*

	Manual (n = 48)		Non-manual (n = 44)		Craft (n = 44)	
	1979	1991	1979	1991	1979	1991
Density (%)	89.6	83.6	62.3	50.4	98.8	96.8

Notes:
1. 'Density' defined as union membership as a percentage of full-time employees.
2. Manuals n = 48; one firm had no manual workers; one firm, figures unavailable.
3. Non-manuals n = 44; one firm had no non-manual workers; five firms, figures unavailable.
4. Craft n = 44; five companies had no craft workers; one company, figures unavailable.

not clustered into individual industry sectors. Nor has any sector remained consistently robust. Take the divisions where manual density is most secure, division 3 (food and brewing) and division 6 (retailing). Division 3 records the steepest reduction in non-manual density, of over twenty percentage points, while division 6 has the sharpest fall in craft density. Put another way, substantial falls in manual density were observed in divisions 4 and 5. For non-manual density, the largest decrease was in divisions 1, 3 and 5, while for craft operatives, the only significant drop is in division 6. Only in division 2 (vehicles and heavy engineering) are substantial falls absent.

Blue-collar trade union presence has remained vigorous. For manuals in 1991 density was above 80 per cent and for craft workers it was above 95 per cent. For white-collar workers the reduction in membership was considerable, although more than half of non-manuals continue to be union members. This trend has been identified in most industry sectors, although there has been little consistency in the distribution of decline. We may compare these figures with previous studies, although considerable caution is again warranted when doing so.

Brown found for manufacturing that 74 per cent of the full-time workforce in workplaces of fifty or more employees were members of a trade union (1981: 51). For manuals this figure was 82 per cent; for non-manuals 48 per cent. This is largely consistent with the 1979 figures in the present study. A reduction in density from 58 per cent in 1984 to 48 per cent in 1990 is established in WIRS (1992: 60). Decline was apparent both for non-manuals and manuals but it was more marked for the latter. Among manuals, the proportion of workplaces having 100 per cent density dropped by half to 14 per cent in 1990. Overall, Millward *et al.* conclude 'the decline in union membership over the period 1984 to 1990 affected the great bulk of industrial sectors and types of workplace' (1992: 62). Again, despite the divergence in sampling and population, a broad trend is evident.

Table 3.2 *Union density by industry sector 1979–1991*

	Manual (n = 48)		Non-manual (n = 44)		Craft (n = 44)	
Sector	1979	1991	1979	1991	1979	1991
1 Energy, minerals, chemicals	98.2	93.2	74.8	56.1	100	97.5
2 Vehicles, shipbuilding, engineering	94.3	88.0	65.1	57.2	100	95.8
3 Food, brewing, tobacco	94.3	92.1	79.3	57.9	100	99.3
4 Rubber, plastics, print	92.9	82.9	48.4	41.7	99.2	98.6
5 Construction, transport, communications	76.7	64.2	72.0	57.6	100	100
6 Distribution (retail, wholesale, film)	73.6	73.3	32.3	26.1	90.0	83.3

Note:
Density defined as union membership as a proportion of full-time employees.

Cases on union density

A number of issues ought to be addressed here, among the most pressing of which is why blue-collar density has remained resolute while white-collar density has diminished. A further concern is what accounts for the reduction in the proportion of 100 per cent unionised workplaces.

Regarding manual union membership, a quite clear explanation comes through from the interviews. F13 is a good example. It is in the energy and chemicals sector. It derecognised a number of craft unions as part of an employment policy of moving away from productivity bargaining and towards individual contracts. But both manual and craft membership rates have remained stable at about 100 per cent:

it is very difficult to translate staff status into a manual culture. It is a protective thing. There is a lack of trust of the company, a fear of the unknown. People believe they can be victimised by management and so retain their union membership.

The firm has been unable to forge a high-trust relationship with craft workers despite a concerted attempt to do so. Distrust of the firm and insecurity about their status is an abiding feature of blue-collar work orientation. F2, in vehicles and engineering, offers a slightly different scenario. Manual density has slipped marginally but remains above 90 per cent:

for individual unionists it is a long-term insurance policy. A strong reservoir of goodwill exists. It is comforting to have an outside organisation. Employees wouldn't naturally dump this. It is a place of security and a means to ensure that fairness is established outside the bargaining arena.

The basis of this reasoning is a positive and strong attachment, a 'reservoir of goodwill' between the workforce and their unions. It is an attachment which in this case supersedes the remoter influences of managerial entreaties and legal reform. The bedrock that continued blue-collar union organisation is founded upon is alienation from the company and its rhetoric and a long-standing affinity with trade unionism. And it is, furthermore, supported by definite practices. F9 falls into the energy and chemicals sector. Manual density is about 98 per cent:

people join because of tradition and peer group pressure. The unions remain strong, confident and active at local level. Also, mills are quite dangerous places.

Scepticism about an employer's commitment to its employees and loyalty to trade unionism are backed by sanctions and peer pressure (in the case of non-compliance) and reinforced by an active local shop stewards organisation. Many other respondents expressed similar attitudes. They suggest that, whatever other changes may have taken place, the disposition of blue-collar workers towards collective organisation remains unaltered, even where unions are no longer recognised for bargaining. There appear to be deep roots in manual workers' frame of reference which ensure that robust trade unionism persists at the workplace.

The picture is less clearly focused for non-manual density. One highly relevant finding is that white-collar unions were more likely to be derecognised than their manual counterparts and this is discussed in the following section. However, it is not clear whether derecognition precipitated a decline in membership or the reverse. At the very least, a number of other factors appeared to be at work. The first is poor union organisation, as at F26, which trades in division 6 (retail distribution). It has a tradition of strong organisation by non-manual unions in its non-distributive subsidiaries. A closed shop existed in 1979 for this non-manual group but, by 1991, density had fallen to around 30 per cent:

the [non-manual] unions have a lazy attitude. They don't have the inclination to devote themselves to members. Union X failed to recognise their members' needs and to adjust their focus. The union does little. Its industrial relations impact is nil.

A lack of animation is the reason advanced here for white-collar density decline. F27 in division 4 (rubber, plastics and publishing) said that poor union leadership was to blame. The main non-manual union, the NUJ, experienced a considerable fall in membership from over 80 per cent to fewer than half of the journalists in the firm:

the NUJ is a chaotic, bankrupt union. The magazine branch is 'anarchist'. The wrong people are attracted to leadership, which is totally unreflective of the membership. Many good people have drifted out or are reluctant to stand for office.

It might be argued that, rather than illustrating the reasons for the shrinkage of white-collar membership, these quotes exhibit the habitual hostility of management to union organisation. But these two cases have been selected because the employers were receptive to unionism and indeed had sought to encourage it and were frustrated at the failure of white-collar unions to retain their membership. In both cases, the white-collar union only was singled out for criticism.

One specific incident best encapsulates this theme. It is mentioned repeatedly to account for the contraction of white-collar density and it is the merger of ASTMS and TASS into MSF. Take F4 in vehicles and engineering: 'many APEX members [subsequently] changed to GMB or went into the wilderness'. F15, in energy and chemicals, underwent a 'dramatic decline':

the merger had a dramatic effect on the morale of [full-time officers] in ASTMS. TASS is more militant and doesn't meet the aspirations of the former ASTMS members. MSF has now lost most of the supervisory grades.

Numerous further examples could be adduced. The primary explanations offered for the diminution in non-manual density rates were that union organisation for these groups lacked any vigour and that the leadership had alienated their members. However, the root of this development may be that white-collar workers identify less strongly with collective organisation than their manual colleagues, and that non-manuals are more disposed to drift out of membership unless they are actively retained. F32 is a prime example in division 4 (rubber, textiles and publishing). Managerial grades in 1979 were a growth area with about 100 members; by 1991 only six remained. It is, the interviewee said, 'now the last thing that comes into their mind'.

Union derecognition

The coverage of collective bargaining has been explored in chapter 2. Of the forty-seven firms which set pay and conditions by joint determination in 1991, five had discontinued doing so by 1991. However, this assessment of coverage was confined to the largest bargaining unit in each panel firm. To evaluate more thoroughly the changing patterns of recognition, smaller, secondary groups of workers also need to be included.

A distinction has been drawn between complete derecognition, where trade union negotiating rights over pay are withdrawn at all establishments and partial derecognition, where negotiation is rescinded for a number of groups but there continues to be at least one union recognised by the firm in question. That is, collective bargaining may be removed for an isolated grade at a single site in a large firm. Or it may be terminated across the firm without exception. A simple taxonomy has been constructed which

Table 3.3 *Union derecognition 1979–1991*

	Number of firms (n = 50)
1 Localised	6
2 Single occupational class	10
3 Multiple occupational class	2
4 All occupational classes	2
No derecognition	30

discriminates between broad changes in the extent of recognition. There are four points on the scale:

1. localised: withdrawal of recognition limited to individual plants or establishments; no firm-wide derecognition;
2. single occupational class: firm-wide derecognition of pay bargaining for a single occupational class;
3. multiple occupational class: firm-wide severance of recognition in a number of but not all occupational classes; and
4. all occupational class: withdrawal of recognition rights in all occupational classes.

There are various potential difficulties with this schema. The first is that all non-corporate-level derecognition is classed as 'localised'. This may underestimate the significance of changes in companies that are decentralised and do not have comprehensive, firm-wide personnel policies. Illustration through case studies offers some compensation for this.

The incidence of derecognition was examined in each firm. Manual, non-manual and craft employees are again separated. Derecognition on the largest scale was recorded. Where, for example, a single occupational class has been derecognised and some localised activity has also occurred, the former takes precedence. Data are displayed at Table 3.3.

In 1979, all fifty firms engaged in collective bargaining to some degree. Even those that did not bargain with the largest unit of workers had negotiations with smaller groups. Some derecognition has been recorded in twenty of these fifty firms, or 40 per cent of the panel. These instances are confined almost entirely to localised events or to a single occupational class. Only rarely have occasions of multiple or complete derecognition been recorded. Derecognition is mainly concentrated among white-collar employees. Non-manuals accounted for all examples of 'localised' termination and six of the ten instances in the 'single occupational class' row. Bargaining rights for manual and craft workers were, by comparison, withdrawn infrequently.

Table 3.4 *Distribution of derecognition across industry sectors 1979–1991*

Sector	1 Local	2 Single class	3 Multi-class	4 All-class	5 No Derecognition
1 Energy, minerals, chemicals	1	3	1	0	3
2 Vehicles, electrical and mechanical engineering	2	0	1	1	9
3 Food, brewing, tobacco	0	4	0	0	3
4 Rubber, plastics, print	2	1	0	0	5
5 Construction, transport, communication	0	.1	0	1	5
6 Distribution (retail, wholesale, film)	1	1	0	0	5
Total	6	10	2	2	30

Presenting these data by industry sector may bring out a further point, which is done in Table 3.4. Only a few numbers in the table need be highlighted. Comparing columns 1 to 4 with column 5, two points may be made. First, the incidence of derecognition is again spread across all industry sectors and, as with the analysis of bargaining levels, no strong clustering of derecognition into certain divisions is evident. Nor are any single types of derecognition – localised, single class, etc. – heavily concentrated into specific industrial sectors. Most sectors evince at least one type of derecognition. This aside, there is a slight bunching of incidents in divisions 1 and 3, where over 50 per cent of firms have experienced some derecognition, mostly of the 'single class' variety.

Summarising this material, 40 per cent of panel firms demonstrated some derecognition, usually limited to 'localised' or a 'single occupational class'. This activity was especially concentrated among non-manual employees. There was no marked distribution by industry sector, with the exception of a faint clustering in divisions 1 and 3. It must once again be stressed that comparison with large-scale surveys is obstructed by differences in sample size and population. The longitudinal data in WIRS suggest a very low incidence of 'full' derecognition. Only '3 per cent of workplaces without any recognised unions in 1990 had previously recognised unions in the period 1984 to 1990. This amounted to just over 1 per cent of all workplaces in 1990' (Millward *et al.* 1992: 74). For private sector workplaces, the figure was even lower.

In the panel of trading sector workplaces, WIRS identified a 'clear preponderance of derecognition' with 'nearly one-fifth of workplaces that reported recognised unions in 1984 reported no recognised unions in 1990' (1992: 75). Yet these episodes were a feature of small engineering establishments where union density in 1984 'had been lower than average' and had 'simply withered away through lack of support from employees' (1992: 75). Most of the firms in the present study are large. A much greater scale of 'full' derecognition has been observed in this study, relative to WIRS, although quite clearly the different scale of the two studies may account for their respective findings.

Turning to 'partial' derecognition, WIRS records a substantial fall in the number of workplaces with more than three non-manual unions, from 33 per cent in 1984 to 23 per cent in 1990. But over the whole decade, however, the recorded decline measured just five percentage points. And these instances were confined largely to the public sector. In CLIRS, 19 per cent of firms reported that recognition for negotiating purposes had been partially or wholly withdrawn, more commonly among large, diversified companies and with a preponderance of those in engineering, 'other' manufacturing and distribution (Marginson *et al.* 1993: 5). This trend is congruent with the present study.

To consider the underlying dynamics of change, a number of cases are now surveyed.

Cases on derecognition

Looking first at the stability of recognition, firms justified their reluctance to derecognise in terms that mirror those given for the retention of collective bargaining, considered earlier. A number of employers professed a commitment to maintaining union organisation. F40, in the food and tobacco sector, expresses a distinct creed: 'We remain embedded in the union ethic. If we didn't have unions we would create them.' Although positive intentions do not preclude firms from hostile actions, firms that expressed some support for unionisation were on average less likely to withdraw bargaining rights.

More complex behaviour was evinced at an alternative subset of firms. These firms sent out contradictory signals about their orientation towards joint regulation. Take F12, in vehicles and engineering, which continues to recognise a multiplicity of unions. The official policy stated early in the interview is that there is no need for recognition to be withdrawn: 'multiple unionism doesn't get in the way. Why move to one union when you can get the benefits with three?' But later in the interview a string of drawbacks to multi-unionism are described. Hourly and staff unions refuse to negotiate jointly. There exists 'great tension' between the two camps, even within the general and white-collar section of a single union. Non-manual unions are alert to any suspected erosion of their relative status. Yet the staff unions organise less than half the workforce, adequate justification for derecognition in other comparable firms. The suspicion must be either that F12 has not seriously considered rescinding bargaining rights or it doubts it has the power to do so.

A third point bears upon the susceptibility of non-manual unions to derecognition. It was management policy in a number of companies to be uninterested in union organisation but to repudiate bargaining rights where membership fell to a minority of employees. F43 is in the food and brewing sector:

ours is not a soft management style. We will ruthlessly pursue being an efficient business. We withdrew ASTMS' rights where they couldn't maintain their membership level. We had to. They were not speaking for the majority.

The firm has not been proactive in bringing about the end of joint regulation. Unions continue to be recognised where membership remains high.

An intriguing counterpoint to these cases is provided by F14, in energy and chemicals. It illustrates a quite different managerial approach, to accomplish, deliberately and methodically, the rescinding of collective bargaining for all employees. Each work group has been balloted on whether to preserve joint negotiations or move to individual contracts. So far, staff and some craft workers have opted to end collective bargaining, while manuals have voted against:

we felt that productivity bargaining was finished. It didn't generate good attitudes. We wanted a situation of ongoing change. There was no sense of opposition among management if we wanted to shift the ground towards non-unionism. Among the craft groups, the boilermakers were the first to come out [of bargaining].

There has been a strategic shift in personnel policy. And this in a firm with 100 per cent craft and manual density and a history of forceful opposition from the shopfloor. This example illustrates how an alternative managerial opinion of what is feasible within an existing power relationship may have radically different results for institutional security. It also accounts for the slight gathering of derecognition in divisions 1 and 3 because a number of firms in these sectors followed a similar policy.

The product of resolute management objectives is illustrated most dramatically in F30, in vehicles and engineering. All unions were derecognised by 1991. In 1979 this firm had the standard engineering characteristics of high-density and multiple unionism. It is an informative case:

by 1981, the company was technically bankrupt. The MD instigated a new policy of improving performance and 'investing in people'. We had a massive problem with strikes, political activism and labour discontent. TASS had been amoral, utterly dishonest. The MD wanted the unions out. In 1986 we told them we weren't going to bargain. They held a ballot for strike action but didn't gain enough votes for a mandate.

The basis for these actions is an ideological hostility to all forms of collective organisation, what some authors have termed 'macho' management. Relations were already hostile. The incoming managing director saw to it that trade unionism was ruthlessly expunged.

Marshalling this information, we can begin to trace the contours of derecognition. Terminating bargaining rights for all or most occupational classes is relatively rare, running to fewer than 10 per cent of firms. It occurs most frequently where there exists a corporate personnel policy unsuited to trade unionism or where senior managers are politically hostile to unions. Much more common is derecognition confined to single occupational classes or localised events, occurring where white-collar density has fallen below 50 per cent. It ought to be remembered that the majority of firms had not withdrawn bargaining at all. This may have occurred because firms did not consider the possibility of derecognition, or judged themselves to lack the necessary power to do so, or because they retained a normative commitment to trade union representation.

The closed shop

The closed shop is 'a situation in which employees come to realise that a particular job is to be obtained or retained only if they become or remain members of one of a specified number of trade unions' (McCarthy 1964: 9). The distinction is usually drawn between compulsory membership to obtain ('pre-entry') or retain ('post-entry') employment. Successive Acts of Parliament in the 1980s sought to make unlawful the enforceability of the closed shop. The Employment Act 1990 gave the right of complaint to an industrial tribunal for anyone refused employment on grounds of non-membership of a trade union. As a result, a substantial fall might be expected in the incidence of the closed shop.

Identifying the closed shop in practice can be problematic. It is 'a complex phenomenon traditionally relying largely upon informal social pressures for its existence' (Brown 1981: 54), one that is closely associated with custom and practice and unwritten managerial involvement. Social sanctions are difficult to identify other than through detailed observation at the workplace.

Respondents were asked whether in practice 'any workers have to be union members in order to keep their jobs' (1981: 54). Practice is again recorded in the largest bargaining unit by employment for each firm. Three classes of closed shop – pre-entry, post-entry and 'none' – have been differentiated. This definition includes written, explicit and also unwritten

Table 3.5 *Coverage of the closed shop*

	Manual (n = 50)		Non-manual (n = 50)		Craft (n = 42)	
	1979	1991	1979	1991	1979	1991
Pre-entry	3	2	0	0	29	23
Post-entry	45	31	22	8	12	16
No closed shop	2	17	28	42	1	3

Notes:
1. Closed shop here includes formal written, explicit unwritten and tacit forms.
2. n = 42 for craft groups because seven firms had no sizeable group of craft workers and one response was unusable.

and non-verbally agreed forms of arrangement. Analysing these practices necessarily entails a degree of subjective assessment, and case illustrations are furnished in the following section. Table 3.5 presents these data.

Coverage of the closed shop in 1979 was widespread. Some form of post-entry membership arrangement was found among 90 per cent of panel firms for manual employees and over 40 per cent of firms for non-manuals. Pre-entry shops in 1979 were frequently in force for craft operatives, covering more than 60 per cent of the panel. The extent of the closed shop has certainly contracted, especially among non-manual groups. The vast majority of white-collar bargaining units no longer have union membership arrangements in force. But, for manuals, the closed shop does remain extant in the majority of units, as does the pre-entry shop for craft workers, although the incidence of both has declined.

Before an accurate assessment may be made, we need to look at the composition of the closed shop, since in addition to written agreements our definition encompassed 'explicit unwritten' and 'tacit' forms. For example, the obligation to join may be enforced verbally by the shop steward and supervisor. Or the requirement to join may not be stated explicitly but is understood by all concerned effectively to be a condition of employment. What interviewees had to say about the form of the closed shop has been collated and summarised in Tables 3.6 and 3.7.

Table 3.6 deals with the formality of the pre-entry shop for craft workers. This took the form in 1979 almost exclusively of an explicit, verbal agreement. There has been a significant shift in formality. The majority of pre-entry shops are now 'tacit' agreements: the practice observed though rarely expressly spoken of. With the structure of the post-entry shop, outlined in Table 3.7, there have also been noteworthy developments. Again the pattern in 1979 is one of highly formalised arrangements. The closed shop for manual and staff workers usually takes the form of a written agreement. Very few of these remain in 1991. For white-collar labour, the formal agreements

Table 3.6 *Formality of
the pre-entry closed shop
for craft operatives*

	1979	1991
Written	0	0
Explicit	28	10
Tacit	1	13

Note:
No cases of pre-entry closed
shop for non-manuals; only
three for manuals.

have been all but extinguished. With manuals, written agreements account for only a small proportion of closed shops, which are now explicit unwritten or more frequently tacit accords. Craft operatives now have no written membership agreements at all.

Looking at the spread of closed shops across industry sectors, a couple of issues may be considered. The craft pre-entry closed shop is more often to be found in divisions such as vehicles and heavy engineering. It is less often present in divisions such as division 3 (food, brewing and tobacco) and division 5 (construction, transport and communication). This distribution has remained in place over time with the exception of division 4 (rubber and print) where its incidence fell appreciably. A comparable trend is evident for the post-entry closed shop. This contracted quite evenly across most industry sectors apart from division 2 (vehicles and heavy engineering) and division 3 (food, brewing and tobacco). Indeed by 1991 these two divisions account for the majority of manual agreements and all but one staff agreement.

Most manual groups in 1979 were regulated by a written, post-entry agreement. Two-thirds continue to be covered but mainly by informal, unwritten accords. The large proportion of craft units in 1979 had an explicit pre-entry shop. Many of these shops survive in 1991 but there has been a shift in form from 'explicit' to 'tacit'. The closed shop for staff groups has been considerably eroded. The contraction of the closed shop has occurred in most industry sectors. It remains most robust in vehicles, engineering, food, brewing and tobacco.

These figures are much higher than those found by the Warwick team in 1978–9. Closed shops occurred for manual workers in 29 per cent and for non-manuals in 6 per cent of establishments (Brown 1981: 54). As has previously been mentioned, there is no reason why the findings should equate given the inconsistent sample populations. But the Warwick authors do

Table 3.7 *Formality of post-entry closed shop*

	Manual		Non-manual		Craft	
	1979	1991	1979	1991	1979	1991
Written	36	6	21	5	7	0
Explicit	8	10	1	0	4	10
Tacit	1	15	0	3	1	6

stress that 'this estimate is derived from employers alone and that, especially where the closed shop arrangements are informal, it will tend to underestimate the extent of the practice' (1981: 54).

The conclusion in WIRS is that 'formal closed shop arrangements became far less numerous' (Millward *et al.* 1992: 98). Sharp reductions were found in the occurrence of both the 'comprehensive' and the 'management strongly recommends' variant of the closed shop. This fall was particularly pronounced among those industries in public ownership in 1984: '90 per cent had a manual closed shop in that year, but less than 1 per cent of those same establishments reported a manual closed shop in 1990' (1992: 98). They conclude that the 'dramatic decline in closed shop arrangements must have arisen largely from the legislative changes of the 1980s' (1992: 99). But this leaves a slight puzzle since nearly half of all workplaces with 100 per cent membership did not have even substantial support from management. Gregg and Yates show that 22 per cent of companies with a closed shop in 1984 had abolished it by 1990 (1991: 366). But nearly a quarter of firms that recognised a trade union were still operating some form of closed shop arrangement in 1990, and three-quarters of companies with a closed shop in 1984 still had some arrangement six years later (1991: 367).

The present study suggests a rather different trend to WIRS and one closer in line to Gregg and Yates (1991). The subset of nationalised industries in WIRS in which the rate of occurrence of the closed shop fell to less than 1 per cent of establishments illustrates this perfectly. Differences in sampling doubtless account for the divergent findings. Possible reasons for this discrepancy may be explored through some short cases.

Cases on the closed shop

The first objective is to authenticate comments made about the closed shop. Labour-supply shops, where management recruits only union-nominated candidates are one of the strongest sources of labour power. They have survived in a number of instances. F14 recruits scaffolders solely from the local

TGWU office. F26, a retail and distribution firm, continues to adhere to the pre-entry arrangements of the film industry:

the labour-supply shop continues because it only affects craft and technical areas and our demand for this labour has reduced substantially.

Practices that are skilled but in total employment terms marginal can survive untouched by legal reforms. As can arrangements that have never been formalised. F41 is in division 3 (food, brewing and tobacco). Its density since 1979 exceeded 90 per cent for both manual and non-manual employees. No formal closed shop agreement has ever been signed and the practice continues unmolested: 'when anyone joins the steward makes himself known and social pressure wins'. Management does not condemn this activity. Indeed, it encourages it because the industry union is 'not militant'.

Yet informality does not always account for the ongoing health of the closed shop. In other circumstances, lack of attention has caused union membership to wane. F4, in vehicles and engineering, in 1979 had a written post-entry shop for manuals with density at about 100 per cent:

it [the agreement] went quietly out of existence. Nobody formally put an end to it. But it has caused manual density to decline to about the mid 60s.

Examples can be found of managerial disinterest both hastening the demise of the closed shop and enabling it to exist untroubled by changes in the law. Informality also creeps into management policy even when there has been a concerted attempt to terminate the closed shop. One example is F37 in retail distribution. In 1979 it had a formal post-entry shop for manuals and an explicit unwritten pre-entry shop for craft workers. Following legislative reform, all reference to the closed shop was deleted. No closed shop is now officially in existence. But SOGAT continues to recruit for the news division in central London, while for manuals the 'actual practice' is still 100 per cent membership.

Compare this with the situation at F34, also in division 6 (distribution). In 1979 it had a detailed post-entry agreement with a number of unions. Following the 1982 Act the manual union decided not to hold a ballot to perpetuate the arrangement because they thought that they would be unlikely to win the required 85 per cent of votes in favour. In 1986 the firm discontinued all closed shop provisions. But with the manual union:

we encourage membership in an underhand way. Those not wanting to join are referred to the union who are allowed to try to persuade them.

Yet the closed shop has not held up and density rates have fallen markedly.

There has been a widespread shift in the distribution and formality of the closed shop but not its total eradication. Union membership arrangements extend across the majority of craft and manual firms in the panel but they have metamorphosed from written arrangements into covert practices, less openly acknowledged, less definite in structure but present even so. The closed shop lives on because it is not worth attacking strategically positioned, highly skilled groups, because it has always been informal, because of managerial endorsement and policy inconsistency. Yet in other contexts, these exact reasons – informality, indifference, support even – have been associated with its decline.

The pattern of the closed shop is more complex than the variables considered above. Employers' intentions are not as powerful an explanatory variable. Certainly, managerial endorsement of the closed shop may enable it to continue in existence. But this must itself be buttressed by an entrenched union ethic, one where union membership is a 'deeply ingrained habit' (Dunn and Wright 1993: 5). Where deep rank and file support has been lacking, the closed shop has tended to go quietly out of existence. Furthermore, it is certainly not true that the law on the closed shop is being widely upheld on the shopfloor. Only exceptionally do managers 'calculate that withdrawing an agreement would make any difference . . . It is more a matter of getting around to complying with the law and the gradual slackening of social enforcement . . . The speed with which this happens appears to depend more on how law abiding the firm feels it ought to be or on the personal values of senior managers or union members' (1993: 24).

Summary

This chapter has reviewed data on a number of features of union security, including union density, derecognition and the closed shop. Analysis of union density found that manual and craft membership rates had remained largely intact but that non-manual density had fallen noticeably. This pattern is re-reinforced by the figures for derecognition, which was especially concentrated among white-collar bargaining groups. The incidence of the closed shop too, had fallen to the greatest degree among non-manuals, although some contraction was also evident among manual and craft groups. The pattern suggested by these data is that collective organisation has remained most pronounced in work arenas where there was a strong ethic of collectivism. There is in certain workplaces an 'ingrained habit' of union membership that is based in distrust of management, fear and of a 'reservoir of goodwill'. Where this disposition is weaker, and where unions are less strongly organised, membership and the collective regulation institutions that are their concomitant are prone to wane.

A number of the main procedural features of work regulation have now been reviewed. These include indices of collective bargaining such as coverage and the level of pay determination, and issues of union security such as density, derecognition and the closed shop. The next chapter turns to substantive issues of work organisation.

4   Work organisation

Attention thus far has focused mainly upon collective-bargaining procedures and collective organisation. The suggestion is that trade union organisation among manual and craft workers at firm level has tended to remain robust. But among workers where an ethic of collectivism is less well entrenched, such as white-collar workers, union organisation has been more susceptible to erosion. We now turn to substantive issues, such as work organisation. The Introduction noted the evidence of a far-reaching change to working practices, including the implementation of more efficient levels of staffing and the removal of union job controls over labour allocation and the quantity of output. In the present chapter, we consider the broad pattern of change in working practices among panel firms, as reported by interviewees, and make some tentative comments upon the different degrees of change among panel firms.

In the firm-level interviews, a number of questions were asked about work organisation. Only the briefest sketch of working practices is included in the 1979 reports, so the narratives are retrospective in scope. But because most panel firms in 1979 were concentrated in the highly unionised sectors of the economy, they typically had numerous labour practices, such as the pre-entry, closed shop in common. This provides some basis for comparison.

Classification of extent of change in work organisation

Work organisation is multi-faceted, and changes to working practices may refer to a wide range of issues, including staffing levels, new technology, controls on recruitment such as the pre-entry closed shop, or rules on labour allocation, such as demarcation lines. As in previous sections, a 'grounded' research method was followed. Changes in work organisation were examined in a random sample of ten panel companies, and the identified reforms were synthesised into a single classification. This produced eight categories of change, which are detailed in Table 4.1. This classification was then used to analyse changes in panel firms.

Table 4.1 *Classification of change in work organisation*

Change	Description
1 New technology	Computer numerical controlled machinery; robot technology; flexible manufacturing systems; computerised process control; computer-aided design/computer automated manufacturing (CAD/CAM); automated warehousing; electronic point of sale (EPOS).
2 Production system redesign	High-involvement work systems, including autonomous work groups; total quality management; lean production; just-in-time manufacturing.
3 Reduction in the number of job grades	Reduction in the number of grades in job hierarchy.
4 Job flexibility	Incorporation of additional duties, e.g. minor maintenance/administrative tasks into operator's role; reduction in the number of job roles at workplace.
5 Working time	Change to shift patterns; move to 24-hour/continuous operation; reduction in the length of the working week of one hour or more.
6 Employee communications	Introduction of employee briefing groups, attitude surveys, consultative committees, feedback loops.
7 Job controls	Pre-entry closed shop; promotion according to seniority/length of service; controls on labour effort; demarcations between staff of differing crafts/skills.
8 Staffing levels	Reduction in the number of staff in the production process; reduction in the number of staff on any one task.

The first category is the introduction of new technology, which refers to all manner of new plant and machinery. In manufacturing, relevant developments include the use of computerised machine tools and computer-controlled manufacturing processes. In retailing, electronic point of sale (EPOS) technology has permitted the development of integrated systems of pricing, stocktaking and warehousing. New technology may be introduced with a variety of strategic intentions, including reducing operating costs, increasing flexibility, improving the quality of a good or service and increased control or integration (Child 1984: 248).

The second category is change to the design of the production system. This refers to the introduction of changes at the level of the workgroup. Such changes may include the implementation of 'high involvement' work systems, where the primary work group is afforded some autonomy from first line management. Other examples of production system reform include lean production, denoted by organisation of labour into teams which may remain closely supervised by first line management, and where the aim is to eliminate defects and remove inventory buffers between the different units of the manufacturing process (Klein 1991).

A reduction in the number of grades in a work hierarchy is the third category. Capelli and McKersie (1987) refer to 'vertical' workrules, or the hierarchy that governs the work system (1987: 445–7). One of the much reported developments in the 1980s was the collapsing of tall hierarchies into flatter structures. This may occur, for example, where a single class of operative is divided into a multiplicity of different grades, depending upon seniority and skill levels, which are then reduced to a small number of grades or even a single grade. For example, Dunn and Wright (1994: 36) found that the Ford manual collective agreement of 1979 included five grades of labour with twenty-one separate subdivisions, giving a total of 577 separate job categories; by 1990, the agreement included five grades but no subdivisions.

The fourth category is increased job flexibility. Capelli and McKersie (1987) differentiate 'vertical' from 'horizontal' workrules, the tasks that are assigned to individual jobs. Horizontal rules may be redesigned chiefly by broadening task specialisation. Job 'rotation' involves shifting jobholders between successive tasks, while job 'enlargement' combines two or more tasks into a single job. A good example of the latter is the development of the 'all-purpose' operative at Cadburys (Smith *et al.* 1990: 326). Other forms of horizontal job redesign may be rather more mundane, for example where workers are required to take on additional ancillary tasks, such as cleaning, along with their usual duties.

The fifth category is change in working hours. Pressure for increased output, or the need to respond more rapidly to customer orders, may require a change in the pattern of the working week. For example, to recover the costs of introducing new technology, production may have to be increased, which may necessitate additional overtime, or an alteration to the system of shift working.

Employee communications mechanisms may be an essential element of workplace restructuring, and this is the sixth category of change. Workplace change programmes such as teamworking and cellular manufacturing often place great stress upon improving flows of information between production operatives and management. This may be achieved through various media, including employee briefing groups, attitude surveys, joint consultative committees and employee suggestion schemes and feedback loops.

The seventh class of change is job controls, which exist in a 'bewildering variety of rights and claims' (Goodrich 1920: 18). One common type is group output norms, which are collectively evolved limits over how much output should be produced, over line speeds or the expenditure of effort in work study trials (Roethlisberger and Dickson 1939). A second set of controls opposes direct managerial command of the labour process, such as the refusal to allow 'policing' by foremen (Goodrich 1920: 137) or opposition to the use of stop watches by work study engineers (Brown 1973: 94). A third set of controls involves labour recruitment, particularly the pre-entry closed shop. This section concentrates upon the 'labour supply' closed shop, whereby a union acts as sole supplier of labour to a firm or industry (Dunn and Gennard 1984: 35). Small labour supply shops could be found in many panel firms in 1979, in sectors as diverse as brewing (drivers), energy and water (scaffolders) or retail (newspaper distribution). The final type of job control refers to restrictions on the mobility of labour along lines demarcated according to craft or skill. Managers are often knowledgeable about such practices because they have been involved in negotiating flexibility agreements. Attempts to end craft demarcations were a high priority of work reform at Cadbury's (Smith *et al.* 1990: 325). But they are not always successful. Ahlstrand relates how Esso attempted to remove restrictions based in custom but that 'very few of the flexibility items were ever really implemented' (1990: 152).

The eighth category of change is to staffing levels. One form of adaptive response to competitive crisis is to raise 'production standards', to increase output as a proportion of factor inputs (Capelli and McKersie 1987: 449). This may be done by rationalising working practices, by reducing operating costs or improving efficiency. The number of workers needed to perform a task may be reduced by reorganising the shopfloor or, for example, by cutting down on absenteeism. Investing in new plant and technology may also increase output per person.

Only specific examples of work reform were recorded, which were either cited as illustrations by interviewees or codified in written agreements. General intentions, such as F5's aim to 'encourage consultation', were excluded.

Extent of change in work organisation

Table 4.2 reports the number of firms which reported one or more instances of each category of change to work organisation. For example, increased

Table 4.2 *Extent of change in work organisation*

Change	Number of firms
1 New technology	15
2 Production system redesign	18
3 Reduction in number of job grades	22
4 Increased job flexibility	27
5 Working time	22
6 Employee communications	10
7 Job controls	17
8 Staffing levels	22

Note:
n = 50 firms

job flexibility was the most commonly recorded change, with twenty-seven firms reporting at least one example. This was followed by a reduction in the number of grades in the job hierarchy, changes to working time and reform of staffing levels, for each of which twenty-two panel firms recorded one or more instance. An example of production system redesign was found in eighteen firms, followed by the introduction of new technology in fifteen companies, employee communications reform in ten firms and the revision of job control in seven firms.

As an illustration, some examples of change follow.

New technology

F11 and F12, both vehicle manufacturers, had introduced various forms of computerised automation on their production processes. At F27, a printing and publishing firm, compositors were replaced by new 'front end' systems which permitted direct entry of print by journalists. At F29, a printing and stationery firm, a new printing press was installed, which led in turn to tighter staffing levels and continuous production. F33, a retailer, introduced EPOS terminals, while F35, another retailer, had introduced a computerised sales and stock control system.

Production system redesign

F1, a manufacturing company, had introduced TQM in its main operation. At F2 and at F5, both engineering and electronics companies, and at F11, a vehicle manufacturer, cell manufacturing had been established. Another engineering company, F4, had implemented TQM across each of its manufacturing sites. At F9, teams were introduced on a plant basis, with plants adopting the principle and implementing the model as they saw fit. Teamworking was installed at F6, a cable manufacturer, while F12, a vehicle manufacturer, had introduced quality manufacturing in a series of stages.

Reduction in the number of job grades

At F15, an oils company, the separate grading structures for craft, manual and clerical staff were integrated into a common system at one refinery. At the other refinery, operator grades were reduced from fifteen to seven, and a single craft grade was introduced. Single status with standardised conditions of employment for all non-managerial employees, together with a single grade of production operative, was implemented at F40, in the food manufacturing sector. At F44, in the engineering and electronics sector, its telecoms division moved from a ten-grade to a six-grade structure, while at F50, in the transport sector, the common grading system was reduced from ninety to fifty jobs in 1986, using a revised job evaluation scheme.

Increased job flexibility

At F2, in electronics and engineering, there was some cross-skilling of electricians and mechanics. At F5, the EETPU union signed a single union agreement, and the transition to cell manufacturing made the previous skill demarcations largely irrelevant, since there was cross-skilling of all cell members. Some demarcations remained, 'where it makes sense', according to the personnel manager. For example, electricians were not converted to work as machine operators. At F8, another heavy manufacturer, production workers were reported to carry out 'much more maintenance than 10 years ago', according to our interviewees, with 'total integration' of craft and production operatives. A series of initiatives were launched at F11, including agreements to promote greater occupational and trade flexibility.

Working time

Changes in working time often accompanied the restructuring of work organisation. At F14, an oils company, a new five-crew shift system was introduced, as part of a broader package of changes aimed at increasing job mobility. At F15, another oils company, the work week was reduced from forty to thirty-seven-and-a-half hours in 1981, as part of a package of measures to change working practices and lower costs. Five-shift working was also introduced at one refinery in 1985. With F25, in the transport sector, an agreement was drawn up in 1981 and consolidated in 1982 which permitted the working day to vary within pre-set limits, according to the scheduling of services. At F27, in printing and publishing, the union rule that the working day end at 4.15 p.m. was repudiated by management, and replaced by a dual-shift system.

Communication

Various forms of communication device were introduced among panel firms. At F37, a retailer, climate surveys in which all sales staff are asked to comment on their job satisfaction and on their immediate manager were introduced. F4, an engineering company, implemented a company works council with four union representatives. F6, in the construction sector, introduced a central company consultative committee, and also site consultative committees. It also displaced communications through shop stewards with team briefing at its manufacturing plants. F8, in the minerals and chemicals processing sector, also introduced employee briefing by management, although our interviewees suggested that this was 'going stale'. Another food manufacturer had installed a company policy that each manager was expected to cascade information to the shopfloor.

Job controls

F36, a retailer, indicated that numerous restrictive practices had been uprooted. There was an end to 'job and finish' among delivery staff in 1984, with an afternoon shift introduced, and bonus rates based on speed of delivery replaced by a single consolidated payment. F2 put an end to the system of craftsman's 'mate', whereby union rules specified that each craft operative must be accompanied by a manual worker to assist with job tasks. At F9, management took steps to reduce 'unnecessary' overtime, and also to implement promotion based on ability rather than seniority. At F20, a food manufacturer, some promotion by seniority remained, according to the interviewee, but such practices had become 'much weaker'.

Staffing levels

Widespread reductions in staffing levels were reported. Examples are legion. F21, a chemicals company, reported a 33–40 per cent reduction in labour in its fibres division in 1981. At F22, in transport, single rather than dual-manned vehicles were implemented in 1981. F28, a publisher and printer, was over-manned in 1979, according to its personnel director. It closed its warehouse, making all staff redundant, and then reopened the warehouse with lower levels of staffing. F29 took a tougher bargaining stance when negotiating staffing levels; for example, its 1980 collective agreement specified 'realistic manning levels'.

Overall, there was clearly extensive reform to many aspects of work organisation in panel firms in the 1980s, most notably to job flexibility, staffing levels, a reduction in the number of job grades and to working time. There is some congruence between these figures and the findings of large-scale surveys. Edwards asked whether in the previous two years firms 'had made any changes in working arrangements or introduced any schemes to increase the efficiency of labour utilisation' (1987: 122). Changes to new technology, increased efficiency of existing equipment and flexible working were most frequently reported. Much less often cited were changes to demarcations and 'other trade union restrictions'.

In Table 4.3 the data have been broken down by industry sector. A few points are notable. First, there is a broad distribution of reforms in each industry sector. In every category of change and for each industry sector bar one – employee communications in sector 4, rubber, plastics, print – is an example of work reorganisation recorded. In addition, there appear to be concentrations of reform in particular sectors. In sectors 1, 3 and 4, there is a high incidence of changes to staffing levels. This may reflect the nature of the technology in these industries, such as the introduction of new printing presses in the print sector, or the capital-intensive production systems in chemicals and oil. In sector 3, food, brewing and tobacco, industry unions are more common. These may be weaker than the large, general unions typical in vehicle production and heavy engineering, for example, and less able or prepared to resist job shedding. In sector 2, and in sector 5, construction, transport and communications, there appears to be a high incidence of change in the 'reduced number of job grades' and the 'increased job flexibility' classes. This may be because this sector has historically been strongly unionised, and there may have been a tendency to conclude highly formal collective agreements with large numbers of individual job tasks. In sector 6, retail and wholesale distribution, there was a particular emphasis upon technical change, reflecting the increasing use of new technology such as EPOS terminals.

WIRS asked whether in the last three years firms had reduced demarcations or increased flexibility of working at the establishment. Even within manufacturing, a wide disparity was recorded between the 20 per cent of establishments in vehicles and transport that reported a change and the corresponding figure of 52 per cent in chemicals and fibres (Millward *et al.* 1992: 334). A similar sectional diversity is apparent in this study.

Table 4.3: *Extent of change in work organisation, by sector*

Change	1 Energy, minerals, chemicals	2 Vehicles, shipbuilding, engineering	3 Food, brewing, tobacco	4 Rubber, plastics, print	5 Construction, transport, communications	6 Distribution: retail, wholesale, film
1 New technology	1	4	3	2	1	4
2 Production system redesign	2	6	4	2	2	2
3 Reduction in number of job grades	5	5	2	2	4	4
4 Increased job flexibility	6	9	4	3	4	1
5 Working time	4	8	2	4	2	2
6 Employee communications	3	2	1	0	3	1
7 Job controls	1	1	1	2	1	1
8 Staffing levels	6	2	6	5	2	1

Note:
n = 50 firms

Table 4.4 *Number of categories of*
work organisation in which examples of
change were reported

Number of categories	Number of firms
0	7
1	4
2	7
3	14
4	9
5	7
6	2
7	0
8	0

Note:
n = 50 firms

Number of changes in work organisation

Table 4.4 details the number of categories of change reported for panel firms. These range from zero changes, to instances of change in six of the eight categories of work reorganisation which were examined. One of the main points to note is the diversity apparent within panel firms. In seven firms, no major examples of work restructuring were observed. In a further four cases, only in one category of work reform was a change registered, and in an additional seven firms, the equivalent figure was a mere two. The median figure is three categories of change, into which fourteen firms fall, followed by an additional nine firms with change in four classes. Finally, seven firms demonstrated reforms in five categories, and a further two firms indicated examples of change in six of the eight classes. There were no firms with examples of changes in seven or the full eight categories.

Evidently, quite different degrees of work organisation were apparent among panel firms. One question is whether this trend varied according to industry sector. Table 4.4 sets out these data. Only perhaps in sector 6, which includes retailing, is a marked sectoral distribution evident. Two of the seven firms in this sector recorded zero changes, while no firms were found to have five or six changes. However, as the table shows clearly, the most notable trend is the wide variation in the number of classes of change observed in each sector. For example, in sector 2, vehicles and heavy engineering, there are examples of firms in every category, from zero changes, to one firm which registered change in six categories. In sector 1, oils, chemicals and utilities, there are no companies with zero or one change, but there

Table 4.5 *Number of categories of work organisation in which examples of change were reported, by sector*

Number of categories	Energy, minerals, chemicals	Vehicles, shipbuilding, engineering	Food, brewing, tobacco	Rubber, plastics, print	Construction, transport, communications	Distribution: tail, wholesale, film
0	0	2	1	0	2	2
1	0	1	1	2	0	0
2	1	2	0	3	1	0
3	4	4	0	1	1	4
4	2	1	3	1	1	1
5	0	2	2	1	2	0
6	1	1	0	0	0	0
Total	8	13	7	8	7	7

Note:
n = 50 firms

is a range from one company with change in two classes, to a single company with change in six classes. Sector 5, construction, transport and communications, evinces a similar trend. Two companies have zero change, and two companies demonstrate change in five classes, with a single company in each of the 'two', 'three' and 'four' change categories.

It is necessary to illustrate the trends outlined above with some examples. The first is F3, a manufacturer of cables and other construction industry equipment. This firm recorded no major changes to work organisation. According to our interviewee, it continues to be 'very traditional' in job design and employee communications. There have been no major reforms in either area. It is admittedly 'backward' at TQM. The interviewee mentioned some examples of isolated pockets of change, although these did not register on the scales employed in the previous section. The company's two plants now no longer have full-time convenors, and the job cuts of the early 1980s left supervisory staff feeling more empowered: job losses 'made foremen think they were God', said the personnel manager.

F10 is in sector 2 (vehicles and engineering) and recorded change in one category, to its hours of work. In 1981, an early retirement provision was concluded, and the unions agreed to consider a reduction in overtime. This was followed in 1985 by a change to working time, whereby a number of hours in the work week could be 'banked' and later taken as holidays. There was a further change, as CAD (computer aided design) workers moved to shift work. In 1987, production workers voluntarily accepted a pay cut, of £20 per week, to reduce operating costs. Management announced a round of redundancies and then withdrew it, following a threat of industrial action. In 1990, there was an attempt by management to specify 'minimum' rates of productivity across the plant.

But by 1991, there continued to be three full-time union convenors, a number which had remained unchanged despite the fall in the total employed workforce. Production was organised into 'gangs', who controlled output and labour allocation. Workers could not be allocated to a gang without their agreement. There was also resistance to movement of labour across union boundaries. Because production gangs controlled output, management could not alter the speed of the production track. At the time of our interview in 1991, management had negotiated the introduction of measured day work to replace piecework, which was perceived by management to be the source of the power of production gangs. But following twenty-three meetings, after which an agreement about measured day work was finally reached, the unions refused to implement the deal, according to management, citing differences of interpretation. Management then sought to impose the deal, which provoked shopfloor into 'downing tools'.

In certain cases, the scale applied above indicates limited change, but the reforms that were actually implemented had quite profound consequences for the organisation of work. Such a case is F8, a communications company, located in sector 5, which registered change in two categories. In 1979, all staff were represented by trade unions. There was a civil-service type grading structure, with a large number of individual grades and a formal job evaluation system. This was replaced by a single band of individual contracts, with pay determined on an individual basis according to performance evaluation by supervisor.

While change to work organisation was commonplace among panel firms during the period of study, there remained in certain companies areas of work which continued to be heavily regulated, if not unilaterally controlled, by unions. F13, an oil company, recorded reforms in three classes – staffing levels, flexibility and working hours. It had engaged in a sustained attempt to drive out 'restrictive practices'. In 1980, the labour productivity target at one refinery was increased by 15 per cent. It was followed in 1981 by an agreed productivity scheme with the TGWU, in which management and union representatives visited the company's refining sites to seek means of raising production efficiency. An agreement to implement voluntary redundancies was reached in 1983, and followed by a site agreement in 1984, which stipulated the abolition of demarcations, and the introduction of 'flexible craftsmen'. By 1991, the white-collar trade union had been derecognised due to a 'lack of interest' from the membership, according to our interviewee. But at refinery level, closed shops continued, partly due to tradition ('our apprentices know what the system is'), and partly due to informal coercion, what the interviewee termed the 'behind the bikesheds' method of enforcement. Craft operatives had been shifted onto staff status, and with it had come 'greater flexibility'. As the number of employees had declined, workers had to work 'much harder'. But demarcations remain strictly enforced. If a piece of pipe needs to be moved, two riggers must be sent even if it is moved using a fork lift truck. Boilermakers recently went on strike for six consecutive days because electricians had used angle iron. Subcontractors have adopted custom and practice.

It is also important to show how a small number of changes in working practices could markedly affect production outcomes. F17, a rubber and tyre manufacturer, recorded changes in three categories of work organisation. According to the interviewee, the firm in 1991 had 'in real terms about half' the number of employees of 1979. Total person-hours worked had been cut from 25,000 to 15,000 during this time. Using work-study techniques, these cuts in staffing had been combined with increases in process output of 61 per cent, much of which was concentrated in the late 1980s. Labour productivity had increased from 3.79 to 6.1 units per person during the period of reference. Practices such as 'job and finish', whereby employees may leave work before the official end of the working day if their work has been completed, had been eradicated. These efficiency improvements occurred at the expense of increased wastage. The 'total internal failure bill', i.e. scrap, had increased in real terms from £50,000 to £85,000 per week during the late 1980s. Importantly, there was a sea change in management's attitude to securing work reforms. Where previously, according to our interviewee, management had been 'dominated' by trade unions, and had 'asked permission' to change work practices, by the late 1980s there was a quite different management culture, whereby change was not negotiated but imposed.

At F16, an engineering company, there was a similar story of a shift towards greater managerial prerogative. The company acquired a manufacturer of rubber goods, which had traditional multi-union plant-level representation, including several pre-entry closed shops. Union activities had been co-ordinated from a bungalow in the middle of the site. The incoming management bulldozed this building, the symbol of union power at the plant, and returned the shop stewards to full-time work.

Reforms in four categories of work organisation were identified at F31, a paper and print firm. This company in 1979 established a new paper mill which incorporated a change in shift pattern, tighter manning arrangements, flexible work practices, new technology and an average pay increase of 35 per cent upon rates specified in the national agreement. These new methods then influenced bargaining in the company's other brownfield sites. Our interviewee reported fewer restrictive practices, which in part was related to the elimination of piecework, and the reduced scope for labour control of output. Management claimed that productivity increments were due to greater investment in equipment, rather than to increased effort, but they also noted that the 'idle men have gone' and the 'unproductive' parts of the company were shut down.

At F40, a food manufacturing and beverage firm, five of the categories of work reorganisation were filled. At this company, there had been a rolling programme of work reform. In 1979, a job security agreement was reached, which aimed to avoid redundancies. An accord to introduce new technology, and flexible working was agreed in 1980, together with plant speed increases and efficiency reforms at one plant. Also, in 1980, the company implemented single status for its entire non-managerial staff, and standardised their conditions of employment. Efforts were also made to revise the work practices of skilled workers. In 1982, a craft agreement abolished traditional demarcations between workers of different crafts, and it was agreed that craft operatives would report to non-craft supervisors. Flexibility was extended to the demarcation between craft operatives and their unskilled 'mates' in 1984, followed in 1990 by a single site agreement at one factory to introduce incentive pay related to the amount of waste reduction. As with a number of the above cases, the impression given by the management interviewee was one of a shift in the frontier of control. In 1979, he argued, industrial relations was 'out of control'. The unions could 'hold the company to ransom'. Unions were 'running the business' and management was 'reinforcing this through its own behaviour'. Since then, there has been a huge rationalisation. For example, in the bottling operations, the number of staff was halved and £50 million was invested in new equipment. That plant, management claims, is now the 'fastest' producer in the industry. Company-wide consultation arrangements were dismantled and replaced by site-level communications and employee briefing. Quality management was introduced at each point of the production process, including the percentage of work produced without defects, and the number of customer complaints. Performance standards are now defined for every function. But there remain areas of demarcation.

Summary

This chapter has reviewed the major changes to work organisation identified within panel firms. It has shown that changes to work organisation were widespread, with the most common reforms being increased job flexibility, changes to working time, staffing levels and a reduction in the number of job grades, followed by production system redesign and the introduction of new technology. The least often recorded categories were employee communications and union job controls.

Firms diverged widely in the number of categories of change which were recorded. Case study data also suggest a wide disparity in the extent to which firms had confronted job controls and had introduced measures to increase labour productivity. In short, panel companies appeared to differ greatly in how far they had succeeded in shifting the frontier of control. This held even for firms in the same industry sector, and with similar unionisation and other characteristics, and for identical work practices. For example, the labour supply closed shop, a practice commonly conceded to be a constraint upon efficiency, had in certain firms been eradicated but in other firms continued unchecked.

Having considered the procedural and substantive elements of change in panel firms, we next turn to evidence from employers' associations.

5   Employers' associations

Employers' associations are one of the critical institutions of the British industrial relations system. They are defined as organisations 'wholly or mainly of employers and individual proprietors . . . whose principal purposes include the regulation of relations between employers . . . and workers or trade unions' (Sisson 1983: 121). In addition to collective bargaining at multi-employer or national level, employers' associations also mediate in industrial disputes, provide advice and consultation to members and make representations to government and other interested parties. They have in many industries been of key importance in establishing and furthering the regulation of the employment relationship through joint determination.

Multi-employer collective agreements may serve a number of purposes for assenting companies. First, the negotiation by employers' associations of minimum rates of pay and an annual national increment may set a norm for subsequent company bargaining, and thereby reduce the uncertainty of these negotiations. Secondly, industry-wide disputes procedures and associated machinery may constitute an important framework for the resolution of industrial conflict within companies. Thirdly, the provision by the association of advice and mediation services in instances of possible disruption may also be of assistance to member firms.

It might be argued that, where the bargaining power of labour collapsed in the 1980s, company members might be more prepared to withdraw from their associations. There have certainly been reports of the withdrawal of employers and the subsequent breakdown of associations in sectors such as ports, television, in the clearing banks and among multiple food retailers. But there have been few broader studies of the state of employers' associations, and for this we turn to the following data.

The title of employers' associations

Chapter 2 showed that the fifteen employers' associations included in the present study cover a similar range of industry sectors to the companies described earlier, although the employers' associations were heavily con-

Table 5.1 *Change in the title of employers' associations 1979–1990*

	Number
Title unchanged	10
Title changed	5

centrated in the rubber, textiles, plastics, print and paper sector. One means of testing the comparability of employers' organisations is simply to look at their names (Table 5.1). Where associations have experienced major difficulties, such as the ending of collective bargaining and operating solely as a trade association, they have usually altered their titles. A high proportion of associations, one-third, had changed their name, indicating perhaps a considerable degree of discontinuity, compared to a mere 10 per cent of firms that had done so. Of the five units displaying change, three fell into division 3 (rubber, textiles and printing). All were in areas with high labour turnover and relatively poor union organisation such as textiles, construction and retail distribution.

Name-change came about in each case as a consequence of a marked shift in the organisation's functions. At EA10 in distribution, collective bargaining was discontinued and the two industry bodies merged to form a single non-negotiating trade association. With EA7 in textiles, rubber and printing, national bargaining was devolved to district and local bodies, with the association continuing to act only as a co-ordinating and representative organisation. There has been a good deal of restructuring among the panel of associations.

The role and functions of employers' associations

We may start to examine whether associations are moving away from their traditional role as regulators of labour and evolving new functions, such as trade representation and business consultancy. Collective bargaining is considered in the following section. Two sets of issues have been examined here. First, what might be termed the 'traditional' subjects: advice on the law, on industrial relations, the lobbying of the industries' interests to government and other relevant parties. Secondly, services such as management consultancy or administering a labour exchange for industry-approved employees. Table 5.2 presents the findings.

Activities in 1979 were mainly those of the 'traditional' type, such as

Table 5.2 *Functions of employers' associations 1979–1990*

Function	Number in 1979 (n = 15)	Number in 1990 (n = 15)
Legislation	13	12
Government representation	15	15
Industrial relations	13	11
Labour exchange	0	1
Personnel consultancy	1	2
Business consultancy	0	2

advice on the law, on employment and representation. These continue to be the mainstay of the associations' work, despite some contraction in them. There has been some growth in new functions such as business consultancy. One association has formed a labour exchange to supply workers. But these activities tend to be restricted in their scope and, in functional terms, associations in 1990 continued much as before.

Such crude categorisation may obscure change in the style and culture of employers' organisations and indeed we found numerous examples of change of this type. EA15, for example, in division 1 (energy, chemicals, engineering), performs tasks similar in scope to those in 1979 but with a different emphasis:

in 1979 our advisory role focused on the reform of in-company union arrangements – the elimination of fragmented bargaining, synchronisation of review dates and protection of management prerogative. Since then we have expanded our advice into commercial and economic areas, into strategic planning and European issues.

This is a similar mode of operation then, in terms of the provision of advice, but expanded into financial and managerial issues in addition to the established labour relations role. By comparison, the functional scope of EA5 has been considerably altered:

the [association] is run on a more profit-centred basis than in the 1970s. We now do consultancy at £X per hour. This consultancy is undertaken in-company rather than out of management's authority.

Multi-employer bargaining in this body has been greatly undermined. The association has turned itself into a quasi-consultancy, offering not only advice but also the operationalisation of a range of personnel packages at the workplace and its internal structure has been reorganised to reflect this.

The significance of these services ought not be underestimated. Brown's survey found that a high proportion of members were able to draw on advice from their associations. Services on labour law were available to 79 per cent of members, on incomes policy to 70 per cent. Moreover, use of these facilities was reported to be increasing (1981: 21, 23). WIRS also discovered that industrial relations services, such as the involvement of associations in disputes resolution, remained stable during the 1980s and was widespread in sectors such as engineering and construction (Millward *et al.* 1992: 196).

Multi-employer bargaining

Associations commonly undertake multi-employer bargaining. These negotiations may serve a number of purposes. Minimum terms and conditions of employment are often set, with bargainers holding a second, additional round of negotiations within the firm. Alternatively and less frequently, associations may establish rates close to the absolute level of pay in that sector. Government policy during the 1980s, as we have witnessed, was unsympathetic to national pay determination and encouraged firms to set pay to mirror local labour market conditions. Employers were encouraged to decentralise wage negotiations. The extent to which these factors impacted on panel associations may be explored through three rather blunt instruments: whether multi-employer bargaining continued during the 1980s; what proportion of the workforce was covered by it; and how important were the pay rates agreed.

The first issue can be quickly despatched. Twelve of the fifteen associations undertook multi-employer collective bargaining in 1979. One association had abandoned national bargaining in 1978. Two others did not bargain for the majority of workers in the industry but did hold multi-employer negotiations for small groups, such as craft workers. Of the twelve associations bargaining in 1979, ten continued to do so in 1990. One had terminated national negotiations entirely. One persisted only in some regions. A large proportion of those bargaining in 1979 continued to operate some form of national agreement in 1990.

The second issue is what proportion of workers in the industry were covered by multi-employer bargaining arrangements. 'Covered' means abided by the terms and conditions laid out in the national agreement. Employers' associations generally collect information on this subject and extensive data are available in the 1979 reports to aid comparison. But there is no means of assessing the reliability of the figures given. A simple scale of coverage has been applied:

1. over 80 per cent of industry employees covered by the multi-employer agreement;
2. between 60 per cent and 80 per cent of industry employees covered;
3. less than 60 per cent of industry employees covered.

Table 5.3 *Proportion of industry employees
covered by multi-employer bargaining
1979–1990*

Proportion	Number in 1979 (n = 12)	Number in 1990 (n = 11)
more than 80%	8	3
60–80%	4	3
less than 60%	0	5

Notes:
1. Full-time employees only.
2. Three associations not bargaining in 1979, and the
four associations not bargaining in 1990 are excluded.

As with all elementary taxonomies, this is not without difficulties. The
main difficulty entails distinguishing between 'assenting' and 'non-assenting' firms. In some industries, firms are permitted to follow the industry
agreement in all respects except pay and conditions; these are usually
termed 'non-assenting' members. It was not always apparent that non-
assenting members had been discounted in the figures supplied by associations, which would tend to over-estimate the coverage of bargaining.
Results are presented in Table 5.3.

On these figures, there has been a substantial fall in the coverage of pay
and conditions determined at the multi-employer level. Multi-employer
pay in the majority of associations in 1979 extended across over 80 per cent
of the workforce; in 1990 in the majority of cases it extended across less
than 60 per cent. This picture can be supplemented by data on what rates
are established at the multi-employer level. A crude but still helpful distinction is made between 'minima', where the association negotiates a
minimum 'floor' of rates, and 'absolute', or the rates normally paid on the
shopfloor. The distinction between the two is not always transparent and
needs to be based on extensive wage data to be assessed properly. But the
responses of association officials do allow some progress to be made. As
expected, only a small minority of associations bargain 'absolute' pay rates;
most set minimum levels (Table 5.4).

The pattern is one of the majority of associations maintaining multi-
employer bargaining as a means of determining minimum rates, but with
those rates applicable to a greatly reduced proportion of the workforce. If
this were to be examined in terms of absolute employment, it would probably show a still more considerable contraction, because most industries
covered by the study have been shedding labour. This shrinkage is consistent with WIRS3 which identified a 'substantial reduction in the extent to

Table 5.4 *Pay rates negotiated at the multi-employer level*

Rate	Number in 1979 (n = 12)	Number in 1990 (n = 11)
Absolute	2	2
Minima	10	9

Notes:
1. Full-time employees only.
2. Three associations not bargaining in 1979, and the four associations not bargaining in 1990 are excluded.

which there was multi-employer bargaining over rates of pay between 1984 and 1990' (Millward *et al*. 1992: 218).

Why has it occurred? Overwhelmingly, it was the case that large employers had withdrawn from multi-employer bargaining arrangements. Many sizeable firms became 'non-assenting' members of associations. The withdrawal of such firms impacts enormously on industry membership figures. At EA11, for example, in textiles, 90 per cent of industry firms have fewer than 100 employees while the two largest firms account for around 50 per cent of industry employment. Both of these firms rescinded their membership. Their reasons for doing so might be anticipated: 'reorganisation into free-standing business'; the desire to replace piecework with team and modular working; and 'accountability'. These were confirmed in interview with one of the two large firms. This is again consistent with WIRS, which identified a halving in the proportion of establishments that belonged to a multi-employer organisation (Millward *et al*. 1992: 45).

Yet multi-employer negotiations were more enduring than might have been expected. Two-thirds of associations continue to set pay and conditions of some form. Many associations had asked their members whether national negotiations ought to be continued, and, if so, what role they ought to fulfil. EA5, in division 5 (construction and transport) found assenting companies to be 100 per cent in favour; at EA9 in paper, and printing, in 1983 and 1988 members voted 'overwhelmingly' for national negotiations. Conventional reasons for the maintenance of bargaining were again expressed. In competitive sectors such as textiles, where wages average 40 per cent of total cost, multi-employer bargaining 'takes wages out of competition' and 'brings stability'. Another textile association, EA6, finds fear of unions targeting individual firms and seeking 'to spread the highest rate' and also that small companies are conscious of the time spent in negotiations.

Table 5.5 *Membership of employers' associations*

	1979 (n = 50)	1990 (n = 50)
Not a member	16	26
Member of one employers' association	18	18
Member of two employers' association	9	3
Member of three or more employers' association	7	3

This is the logic traditionally used to justify multi-employer bargaining – to ensure a stable and orderly environment, to minimise inter-firm wage bidding and to restrict the bargaining scope of unions. It appears to apply particularly where firms are small, homogenous and geographically concentrated (Commission on Industrial Relations 1972, Sisson 1983: 125). But, despite this continuity, the withdrawal of large firms from industry-wide membership has damaged the security of employers' associations. Brown noted in 1981 that 'in short, there are no signs of a sudden or mass exodus from employers' associations' (1981: 20). By 1990 this could no longer be taken as true.

Company-level data on employers' association membership

Company-level respondents also commented upon membership of employers' associations, and these data are now brought into play. Chapter 2 showed a great reduction in the importance of multi-employer bargaining among panel firms. This section examines whether the trend for companies to devolve pay determination away from the multi-employer level was accompanied by a widespread withdrawal from membership of employers' associations.

Detailed information about membership is available in both time periods. Firms have been classified according to the number of associations of which they were a member. Table 5.5 presents these data. In 1979 around two-thirds of panel firms belonged to an employers' association. About half did so in 1990. The proportion of firms attached to two or more associations also declined sharply.

Studying distribution by industry sector illustrates a number of further points. Most firms that were not members of associations were in divisions 1 (energy and chemicals) and division 3 (food, brewing and tobacco). In division 5 (construction and transport) and division 6 (retail distribution), the majority had been and continued to hold membership. There has been a notable exit from membership in division 2 (vehicles and heavy engineering) and division 4 (rubber, plastics and paper).

Reference to other studies is instructive. That two-thirds of panel firms belonged to multi-employer bodies in 1979 is consistent with Brown's observation of a high level of membership in manufacturing (1981: 19). Millward *et al.* (1992: 45) found that membership had fallen from one-quarter of firms in 1980 to 13 per cent in 1990 but with higher membership rates in engineering (32 per cent), textiles (32 per cent) and construction (75 per cent). This result is also congruent with the present study.

The logic expressed by firms that have terminated membership is similar to that advanced for the devolution of bargaining. Reasons most often cited are the need to achieve 'flexibility' or to reflect 'local market' circumstances. F1, in vehicles and engineering, withdrew from a number of multi-employer associations in the middle of the 1980s:

we brought bargaining in-house to further control, reduce the number of conflict points and to do things on flexibility. We couldn't do deals at national level. The [full-time officers] had a lot of participation in the process but no ownership.

The desire for intra-firm control is the motivating factor here, which echoes the observations of Walsh (1993: 413). At F32, in rubber and printing, the stimulus is hostility to national bargaining. This firm defederated from five associations, each with national bargaining arrangements for manuals:

the nature of the business didn't suit the national bargaining structure. We needed more flexibility in terms and conditions but were constrained by national rates. We wanted to offer more attractive terms but were limited by other federation members. It was impossible to negotiate nationally the productivity and cost reduction factors that we were looking for. Also we wanted a closer identification between management and the workforce, to talk openly and freely.

Internal control over pay and conditions, flexibility demands and the unsuitability of multi-employer bargaining are the factors most often cited as reasons for ceasing to be members of associations.

Over half of panel firms remained members of multi-employer bodies. Again, perhaps the most interesting question is why firms have not followed prevailing fashions. It is not always easy to identify a clear rationale. F34 is in the retail distribution sector. It continues to assent to more than three employers' associations. Quite why is slightly perplexing:

we have carried on bargaining in the same way. We have shown respect to the unions. The national rates in catering are too high but we haven't revoked. We haven't shifted as much as the national climate.

It is difficult to say whether this is a calculated act of retaining the existing bargaining structure or apathy, not getting around to something they ought rationally to have done.

A certain laxity is also apparent in the objectives of F4, in vehicles and engineering. This case is unusual because the firm became a fully federated member of an association only in 1981. The firm's behaviour was stimulated by an attempt in a plant to derecognise a trade union contrary to the wishes of central office. But the underlying objective of this firm was much clearer:

> we have a corporate view on union membership. The firm declared in 1951 that it would recognise genuine trade unionism and this still sets the tone. Forty years of experience has reinforced this philosophy. We are quite ready to deal with unions. There is no anti-union feeling and there never has been.

The firm chose to join the association to minimise the opportunity for future deviance from corporate personnel philosophy.

Check-off

'Check-off' is the automatic deduction of union subscriptions from the employers' payroll. Multi-employer agreements often make a recommendation about the use of check-off procedures. This section investigates any possible change. A simple extant/non extant distinction is made. It refers to collective agreements covering the largest bargaining unit in the industry, usually manual workers. By excluding smaller groups such as white-collar or craft employees it may disguise important areas of change.

Twelve associations recommended the use of check-off among member firms in 1979. The same number did so in 1990. Even in certain instances where associations did not bargain at the multi-employer level, some statement about best practice was made. An example was found of both the termination and the introduction of check-off. One reason for the continued use of check-off was simply that, as with union recognition provisions in chapter 2, it was simply not worth attacking. In certain cases, associations saw some merit in positively supporting the deduction of union dues. EA4, for instance, introduced a commitment to recommend check-off, 'to keep the unions as strong as possible'.

The closed shop

Firm-level interviews suggest a marked contraction in the presence of the closed shop among non-manual workers but for the majority of blue-collar and craft groups the closed shop remains in force as an informal arrangement. The employers' associations in this study are concentrated in industry sectors in which competitive pressures are particularly exacting, and where union organisation is less well established. Change in the closed shop may be examined at a different level of bargaining, and under different organisational conditions, to the company data.

The method adopted is to record union closed shop arrangements for the

Table 5.6 *Incidence and formality of the post-entry closed shop for manual operatives*

Union membership agreements	Number in 1979 (n = 15)	Number in 1990 (n = 15)
Written	6	3
Explicit	1	0
Tacit	2	3
No union membership agreements	6	9

largest bargaining unit, and again this is prone to inaccuracies by over-looking smaller groups of workers. Assessment is based on the 1979 reports, which are rich in detail. These are compared with interviews with senior association officials, supplemented by collective agreements and secondary sources such as the *Industrial Relations Review and Report*. Closed shops are categorised using the approach which was adopted for companies. This distinguishes between the three occupational groups examined previously, between the pre-entry and post-entry closed shop and between three levels of formality – written, explicit and tacit.

A lower proportion of associations record a closed shop, compared with the panel of firms discussed earlier. Table 5.6 outlines the post-entry shop for manuals; Table 5.7 sets out the pre-entry shop for craft workers. No examples were found of a closed shop for white-collar workers. For the largest manual bargaining group, nine of the fifteen associations recorded a closed shop in 1979; six did so in 1990. There was a shift in the formality of the arrangement. Six associations had a written closed shop for manuals in 1979; three did so by 1990, while the number of 'tacit' arrangements increased. And this based on a definition that encompasses formal and informal closed shops. A low incidence of manual union membership arrangements may be due to randomness because of the small number of observations or because the industries concerned, such as textiles, typically are not strongly organised. At the time of the 1979 study, a number of associations were discussing the possibility of introducing a closed shop clause. Alternatively, it may be that association officials are less knowledgeable or inclined to be candid about custom and practice in the industry. For craft bargaining units, eight out of fifteen registered a pre-entry closed shop in 1979, which had fallen to six by 1990. None of these practices were formal, written at either point in time.

Explaining these actions, associations clearly varied in their attitude towards the closed shop and to change in the law. Some associations complied quickly with legal reform, as with EA4, whose formal agreement

Table 5.7 *Incidence and formality of the pre-entry closed shop in craft operatives*

Union membership agreements	1979 (n = 15)	1990 (n = 15)
Written	0	0
Explicit	4	3
Tacit	4	3
No union membership agreements	7	9

'reverted to 100 per cent membership'. At EA2, also in clothing and textiles, there was a much lower degree of conformity: 'the post-entry shop remains in force although the coverage varies. Negotiations are proceeding over the pre-entry shop.' In certain cases, the association had attempted to adhere to the law but with little success. Thus at EA9, in printing and publishing, the craft pre-entry shop continued informally:

the skilled pre-entry shop still prevails. Most workers carry cards and there is pressure not to work with non-members. We advertise in the media but in practice the union is the sole source of labour and controls employment.

Other associations had entirely disregarded legal change. EA8 in rubber and textiles, was sanguine about the continued existence of the closed shop:

the *de facto* closed shop continues to operate, although coverage has declined. There has been no balance of advantage in attacking the closed shop. Unlike say the print industry, no fundamental change has been required in [this] industry.

There is a parallel here with the firm-level data. Where the closed shop had been concluded in 1979, it has in most cases remained in force in 1990, although often informally. Its persistence is due to the indifference or active support displayed by management, to peer group pressure and perhaps to the fact that employers perceive such practices to have little negative effect on performance. Overall, it is the disposition of associations towards the closed shop that is critical in explaining its survival.

Union density

Employers' associations often possess good quality information about the level of union membership within the industry that they represent. Exploring this issue allows us to investigate union density in less well-organised sectors of industry, where unionisation may be more susceptible to decline. There is a detailed breakdown of density in the 1979 reports and the figures given by the associations have been compared with those given

Table 5.8 *Union density*
1979–1990 (industry-level data)

	1979 (n = 14)	1990 (n = 14)
Mean density	64.9	59.6

Notes:
1. In one of the fifteen associations,
data unavailable.
2. Figures refer to union density among
member firms.

by large firms in their constituencies. Unfortunately, density could not be broken down by occupational class. Table 5.8 presents the figures.

Density has declined by five percentage points but remains comfortably above the 50 per cent mark. It is not possible to tell whether this reduction was clustered among any occupational classes. However, it is possible to scrutinise rates of density by industry sector. The steepest decline of over twenty percentage points occurred in division 5 (construction and transport) while division 1 (energy and chemicals) and division 2 (engineering) also recorded marked falls. In division 3 (rubber, textiles and plastics) and division 4 (printing, paper and publishing), density rates were much more stable. One explanation for this pattern could be that derecognition was concentrated in sectors in which density fell more markedly. This pattern may, in turn, be related to the presence of industry unions, which may be less assertive than large, general unions in engineering and to an extent construction.

Union derecognition

Firm level data suggest that the withdrawal of negotiating rights for all unions within a firm was comparatively rare. Localised cases and the derecognition of white-collar unions were much more common. Once again, employers' association officials are frequently well informed about union derecognition among member firms. And it is worthwhile to examine recognition among sectors with different characteristics, such as a preponderance of small firms, geographically concentrated, 'traditionally minded' employers and so on. One might expect firms in these industries to be more readily persuaded of the potential benefits of derecognition.

The responses of association officials are examined and the form of

Table 5.9 *Union derecognition*

	Number (n = 15)
None	7
Localised	4
1–2 firms	1
3–6 firms	3
more than 6 firms	0

Note:
One instance of derecognition refers only
to white-collar unions.

classification is the one employed previously, with minor modifications. It was not possible to separate cases of derecognition according to occupational class. Association officials were usually unaware of highly localised instances of derecognition, such as where negotiation had been terminated for a managerial grade in a single plant of a firm. They were much more knowledgeable about corporate level derecognition and this is the basis of the scale. There are five classes:

1. none: no known occurrences;
2. localised: instances confined to grades or occupational classes within individual firms;
3. derecognition of majority union in one or two industry firms;
4. derecognition of majority union in three to six industry firms; and
5. derecognition of majority union in six or more firms.

Plainly, this taxonomy may underestimate the degree of localised derecognition. It may overlook informal derecognition, where there is no formal ending of the written agreement but negotiations just cease to occur. Accepting these criticisms, we are dealing with sectors where recognition of a single industry union is more common, in which it is less likely that one of a large number of unions could be excluded from bargaining.

Table 5.9 exhibits the data. The majority of associations do report some occurrence of derecognition. Four cases are 'localised'; four are firm-wide. In only a single case does firm-wide derecognition refer to white-collar unions alone; in the three other examples it includes blue-collar unions also. This is ostensibly a considerable softening of union representation among associated firms. But we cannot judge its true significance without reference to the number of firms within the industry. EA4, for example, in textile manufacturing has 230 member firms, of which derecognition in between three and six cases is largely irrelevant. EA7's evidence is instructive:

no real moves forward on derecognition. Firms feel vulnerable to pressure from the general unions – it is a good recruitment area – and most prefer the industry union. Our advice has been to leave things as they are and to avoid disruption: to maintain a calm and peaceful atmosphere.

Rather, derecognition has been confined to the numerically large, high-profile firms, those most likely to exit from industry bargaining procedures. They are insignificant in terms of the total population of firms but considerable no doubt in the total employed.

Summary

The panel of employers' associations examined here covers a variety of industries but is skewed towards the rubber, textiles and plastics division. There is much evidence of major disruption to associations – five of the fifteen studied had changed their title, although most carried out a similar range of functions. In particular, there was much to suggest that multi-employer agreements covered a smaller proportion of industry employees. In around half the cases examined, industry agreements extended across fewer than 60 per cent of industry employees. Large firms had tended to withdraw from membership, citing reasons such as the reorganisation of internal control structures and working practices. Yet two-thirds of associations continue to bargain over wages and conditions and there was considerable evidence that, among smaller companies, the function of stability and taking wages out of competition remains greatly valued.

Other aspects of these industries have also been studied. A lower incidence of the closed shop has been found, compared with the panel of firms, while the spread of the closed shop had contracted during the period of study. But around half of manual and craft bargaining units are still bound by union membership arrangements. Some associations have adhered strictly to the law on the closed shop but in many cases there are clear indications that the closed shop survives informally, or that associations have disregarded legal provisions. Although aggregate density fell by only five percentage points, there was a much higher proportion of derecognition among manual occupations, compared with the firm-level data. There has been some softening of collective bargaining and union representation among the industries examined here but not to the degree where one could convincingly argue that joint regulation has been largely eradicated. This raises the question of what factors have shaped the strength and weakness of collective regulation and this issue is the focus of the following two chapters.

6   Competitive pressures

The preceding chapters focused upon institutional and workrule change, including collective bargaining, union security, work organisation and employers' associations. One key issue raised in the introduction was how environmental pressures conditioned the pattern of institutional change. This chapter examines the nature and effects of competitive pressures and legislative change, as perceived by respondents in panel firms.

The first variable to be considered is the acuteness of product market competition, and the extent to which product market pressures were reported to have intensified in the 1980s. Second, the study will examine the impact of a slump in product market demand on panel firms. Privatisation is the third variable, which by exposing hitherto sheltered firms to the rigours of the market, has also been cited as having a disciplinary effect upon management. The discussion will also encompass the threat or experience of a contested takeover, which may stimulate companies to redesign the hierarchy of rules on the shopfloor

Employment law reforms have also been identified as having a critical effect upon the balance of power in employment relations. Here, we report management responses, on their broad opinions about legal change, on their propensity to apply legislative sanctions against trade unions and on their past use of employment law.

The two variables – product market competition and employment law – are considered in turn.

Competitive conditions

One of the most important subjects for discussion is the competitive conditions endured by companies in the panel. This may be a factor of critical importance accounting for the pattern of industrial relations reform within panel companies. Comments have been compiled on three topics: competition, recession and ownership. It is worth underlining the remark made in a previous chapter, that the intention was not to amass large quantities of statistically pliable data. The following analysis relies chiefly

Table 6.1 *Product market competition*
1979–1991

Rate	Number in 1979 (n = 50)	Number in 1991 (n = 50)
1	28	8
2	20	36
3	2	6

Notes:
Product market competition:
1. 'Limited' competitive threat from other firms in the sector.
2. 'Substantial' but not extreme competitive threat from other sector companies.
3. 'Extreme' competitive threat to the viability of the firm.

upon interviewees' comments, supplemented by material from FT *Profile*, which are placed into broad bands of change and are then illustrated through specific examples. Despite the qualifications that this implies, it is possible to shed light on a number of important issues.

Product market competition

Various studies examine the level of product market competition faced by firms and apply a number of indices to do it. WIRS studied the number of competitors in the market (Millward *et al.* 1992: 12); Edwards asked about the severity of competition (1987: 17); while Marginson *et al.* examined product demand in the previous twelve months (1988: 40). This section examines respondents' comments on competitive pressures. These ranged widely, including issues such as the number of competitors within a market sector, size of market share, ease of market entry etc. An overall assessment was made of each respondent's views, based upon key words and phrases, and firms were placed into a three-point classification. These are illustrated with examples. The 1979 reports afford only limited details about product market competition, and the following information is based mainly on retrospective narrative. Admittedly there is some approximation involved in putting firms into categories but fairly broad bands are used and some cases are shown at the end of this section.

Data are presented in Table 6.1. According to this measure there has been some intensification of product market competition, although not an

Table 6.2 *Matrix of product market competition 1979–1991*

	1991			
	Rate 1	Rate 2	Rate 3	1979 total
1979				
Rate 1	6	21	1	28
Rate 2	2	15	3	20
Rate 3	0	0	2	2
1991				
All rates	8	36	6	

Notes:
n = 50 firms.
Product market competition:
1. 'Limited' competitive threat from other firms in the sector.
2. 'Substantial' but not extreme competitive threat from other sector companies.
3. 'Extreme' competitive threat to the viability of the firm.

extreme change, between 1979 and 1991. Far fewer firms are in rate 1; in rate 2 there has been an appreciable rise. Table 6.2 displays these data in 'matrix' form. This format enables change in the rate of product market competition to be traced in greater detail. For example, of those firms with a '1' rate of competition in 1979, six continued to have a '1' rate in 1991, while twenty-one had a '2' rate and one firm a '3' rate. Similarly, of those firms with a '2' rating in 1979, most continued to warrant that rating in 1991.

There seems to have been only a limited growth in product market competition in this period. Few firms appear to have shifted from having a 'limited' competitive threat to enduring a level of competition that imperils the firm's viability. These figures are at least partly consistent with WIRS, which found a mild increase in the competitiveness of markets between 1984 and 1990. For manufacturing firms with five or more competitors, this increase was 'slight', from 49 per cent to 54 per cent; in services, this increase was greater.

F27 provides an instructive example. This firm is in rubber, publishing and print. It is rated '1' in 1979 and '2' in 1991. Its primary market is magazine publishing and competition has certainly intensified in this sector. The economics of this industry have changed. In 1979 the best-selling magazine had a print run of 400,000 copies per issue, a readership of 4.8m and a lead time of eight weeks. Technological change has obviated the need for compositors; entry costs have been reduced; there has been an 'explosion' in the number of magazines; the circulation of the firm's main title has fallen; and the lead time to printing has been halved. Competition is simply more acute.

Other firms report similar trends. At F1, a packaging and manufacturing company, the interviewee noted 'severe competition' in supplying products to the automotive industry, and a heightening of economic pressure in other sectors, which had resulted in a change in management style. F8, a communications and construction firm, pointed to greater competition which had prompted a re-evaluation of the company's markets. F12, a vehicle manufacturer, noted increased competition from Japanese companies, and the 'realisation that competition is dangerous' which had been 'highly influential' in forcing the company to change its working practices.

In certain cases, there was a distinct sectoral basis to enhanced competition. In the oil industry for instance, all three companies maintained that there was greater rivalry in the market for oil. F15 observed that the industry was increasingly competitive, as refinery technology had become more widely available and lowered barriers to entry. Small, high-technology refineries had created pressure to reduce operating costs, which was exacerbated by surplus refining capacity, and retail competition from supermarkets. Fluctuating oil prices added to the pressure on margins.

Changes in the specification of the product were driving competition in other sectors. The interviewee at F28, a printer and publisher, maintained that the market for books had shrunk in the 1980s, necessitating a move to shorter print runs of 500 copies, which increased average costs. Production costs had to be lower in 1991 than they were five years previously for the company to compete effectively. The food manufacturer, F39, witnessed its principal products being attacked by supermarket own-brands, in a mature market with little scope for growth, which brought about pressure to cut costs. Our interviewee at F9, in sector 1 (chemicals and metals production) observed that in the 1960s there was a high demand for large volumes of second-class metal, whereas in the 1980s, the market had shifted towards higher quality, lighter, stronger metal, with evident implications for the manufacturing process. Similarly, at F18, a construction goods manufacturing company, the growth in the market was away from standardised bricks and towards those with more specialised facings.

In certain sectors, the state had played an important role in extending competition. F29, a state-owned printer and publisher, saw the government's share of its printing work fall from 53 per cent to 20 per cent. Much state printing was awarded to other printers, often from the private sector, including contracts for national savings stamps, post office telephone directories, and printing for the Ministry of Defence. The agency was forced to compete for its orders on commercial terms, as the government emphasised cost factors in allocating printing contracts. Price consequently became more important.

Yet, while a higher proportion of firms claimed that their product market environment was more combative, far fewer said that raised levels of competition had impacted significantly upon the operation of the firm and specifically upon the organisation of work. This is evinced well by F42, in food, brewing and tobacco. This firm similarly was rated '1' in 1979 and '2' in 1991. Its trading sector has indeed become more competitive. Market sales in the 1970s had risen consistently and the firm's objectives were merely to maximise volume throughput. During the 1980s, sales had been declining on average by 3 per cent to 4 per cent per annum, as new products were launched by rivals. Simultaneously, government regulations forced the firm to cut the number of tied sales outlets by almost half, further threatening sales volume. Yet the firm claimed that intensified competition had not provoked an internal crisis:

there has been no major crisis but we are conscious that everybody is vulnerable. We have been the industry leader for a long time and considered ourselves fairly impregnable.

Other companies with dominant market positions concurred. F18, for instance, the construction products manufacturer, held 45 per cent of the UK market for bricks at the time of interview, with a further 50 per cent held by other large producers, and the remaining 5 per cent by smaller firms. As such, its market position was not threatened by competitors, with smaller industry firms tending to be squeezed out of the market. Pressure to reduce costs existed, none the less, due to excess industry capacity and severe cyclical swings in the construction industry. F24, in transport, had the largest market share in the road freight business and competed mainly against four or five smaller companies. F17, the automotive components manufacturer, was a niche player, holding only 4 per cent of the UK market. This firm competed at the high end of the product range, supplying to Rolls Royce, with most of the other industry producers aiming for the high-volume mass market.

The impression given here is of a moderate intensification of product market pressure, which was insufficient to impact substantially on firms' operations. This is in accordance with secondary sources such as WIRS. But we ought to be sceptical about deducing too much from these figures. Competition is about action, rather than market share or the number of participating firms. Ten firms may collude while just two can oppose each other furiously. The rating employed here tends to ignore the dynamics of action. It is also wise to be hesitant about deducing too much from retro-

Table 6.3 *Impact of recession*

	Impact of recession		
	1	2	3
Number of firms affected	8	21	21

Note:
n = 50 firms.
Impact of recession:
1. Limited effect on product demand; profitability
unaltered.
2. Marked decline in market demand 1980–2;
profitability significantly reduced.
3. Sharp fall in market demand 1980–82;
threatened the short-term viability of the firm.

spective comments – there may be a tendency to rationalise the present as more demanding, more compelling than the mundane past. Yet the cases cited do imply that some alteration to competitive conditions has occurred.

Impact of recession

A second feature of the market environment is the effect of recession in product markets and labour markets between 1980 and 1982. The first Conservative administration allowed demand to fall and unemployment to rise and left market agents to adjust their behaviour accordingly. It may be that firms in sectors where the decline in demand was especially steep were impelled to push through changes to work organisation. The method pursued mirrors that used in the previous section. Firms are placed into broad bands of change based upon key words and phrases used in interview. In this section, the main issues concern a fall in product demands and a decline in profits during the period of study. The difficulties in doing so mirror those encountered in the previous section.

Data are presented at Table 6.3. Based on this scale, the large majority of firms reported that, during the recession, profitability had either been significantly reduced or had seriously threatened the commercial viability of their firm. This was accompanied in each case by a fall in the normal levels of product market demand. For over twenty companies the fall was marked. All of these firms made a financial loss. Only eight of fifty companies said that the recession had little or no effect on profits or demand. That recessionary pressure was a more powerful stimulant to change than intensified competition is consonant with alternative data sets. Edwards examined manufacturing firms in 1984. He found that profit as a percentage of turnover had diminished substantially between 1978 and 1982, that the large majority of respondents reported severe or very severe competition in all markets but also 'some evidence that the nadir of the plants' fortunes had been passed' (1987: 17). Marginson *et al.* note that 55 per cent of establishment managers in 1985 had reported rising demand but only 12 per cent reported falling demand (1988: 40).

A number of cases help to animate this picture. F30's sector is vehicles and engineering. It rated '3'. In 1979 it was a public sector monopsonist, having exclusive rights of supply to all branches of government and public companies and doing so on the basis of cost-plus pricing. With the advent of new regulations and with a government spending policy of purchase from the lowest-cost producer, this right was removed. Both public and private sector demand collapsed in the early 1980s. The firm went technically bankrupt, supported by government loans and forced the 'realisation that we couldn't continue, that we were decadent'. System-wide productivity improvements were made from this time on.

In the same division and also rated '3' is F2. It made in 1979 its first financial loss in 120 years, caused by a plunge in product demand. It dates from this event a reversal in its policy stance, in particular a preparedness to divest, to enter into joint ventures and to sell underperforming business which 'twenty years ago we wouldn't have needed to'.

F3, a cables manufacturer, experienced a 'sudden recession' in 1979, which left its rod division with 'enough capacity to supply the entire industry', and which resulted in a 'lot of concessions' in work practices. The automotive components manufacturer, F7, said the demand for car batteries was 'very low' and 'badly hit by the recession'. Another automotive supplier, F17, described a 'massive downturn' in demand for tyres in the early 1980s. One automotive manufacturer, F47, outlined the 'desperate state of the motor industry' in the early 1980s. A similar trend is apparent at F9, a metal manufacturer, which made a £1,200 million loss in the year 1979–80. In the transport sector too, F24 described the recession in 1980–1 as 'especially severe'. Another transport company, F50, made a loss of £100 million in 1981–2.

While the bulk of the panel experienced a sharp downturn in trading conditions in the early 1980s, with negative effects upon profitability, this experience was not universal. The oil companies, in particular, were not as seriously affected as those in sector 2 (vehicles and heavy engineering). One oil company, F13, said that the oil refining industry remained highly profitable, with the emphasis upon sustaining production, such that it was 'never worth fighting a battle'. Another oil firm, F15, costed the closure of a refinery at between £10 million and £20 million per week. The tobacco

Table 6.4 *Status of public sector firms 1979–1991*

	Number in 1979	Number in 1991
Public sector	10	1
Privatised	–	8
Agency status	–	1

company, F41, argued that it had not witnessed the downturn which had affected other sectors. A similar point might also be made for the large retailers.

Ownership

One of the principal correctives to poor performance in the market mechanism is the threat or actuality of takeover by a more efficient competitor. The extension of product market competition is the reason underlying the transference of many public sector corporations from the public to the private sector. This is a relatively easy subject to research. Managers should be well-informed about previous takeover bids or a change in their ownership status and such events are in any case well documented in the specialist press.

Table 6.4 presents some data on the status of public sector firms. One-fifth of panel firms in 1979 were in the public sector. Of these virtually all have been transferred to the private sector. One remains in the public sector; one has 'agency' status, that is it is publicly owned but able to trade as a private firm, distanced from government business restrictions. Surveying the forty firms that were in the private sector in 1979 (Table 6.5), four were privately owned or controlled and could not be the subject of a stock market takeover bid. Of the remaining thirty-six firms, nine or one-quarter of the panel had experienced a bid and six of these had actually been taken over. In each case the aggressor was a large consortium, four of which were British, one French and one from the United States. Taking the whole panel then, 40 per cent of firms had either been privatised or threatened with a takeover and in one-third a forced change in ownership had taken place. There was a good deal of turbulence in the environment of panel firms, particularly regarding their ownership status and the possibility of a hostile takeover.

Privatisation was certainly a force for change in industrial relations. It

Table 6.5 *Ownership of firms in*
the private sector in 1979

Private sector firms in 1979	40
Firms open to a takeover bid	36
Firms subject to a takeover bid	9
Firms actually taken over	6

was noted above that the printer F29, and the electrical goods manufacturer F30, were greatly affected by the withdrawal of their preferential or
exclusive government-supplier status. In other cases, such as the vehicle
manufacturer F11, the government refused to continue underwriting its
operating losses, which created additional pressure to reduce costs. At F25,
a public transport company, the grant for providing commercially non-
viable services was progressively reduced.

Takeover could also provoke radical change. F18, a construction industry goods manufacturer, was acquired by a large conglomerate following a
contested bid. The incoming management altered accounting procedures,
making further investment conditional upon achieving changes to working
practices. F17, the automotive products manufacturer, had 20 per cent of
its shares purchased by a large conglomerate, which then sold them to a
Japanese tyre producer. At F43, the threat of a hostile takeover in 1984
created a climate of 'crisis', according to our interviewee, which stimulated
changes aimed at improving efficiency. With F26, a film distribution
company in 1979, which at that time was making zero returns on its existing business, institutional shareholders' threats to replace senior management spurred reform. Hence, even in those firms that were not threatened
with takeover by a rival firm, capital market pressures powerfully shaped
management behaviour.

Summary

Despite the approximation inherent in these indicators, it is possible to
identify a coherent pattern in the nature of environmental pressure in the
period of study. By 1991 firms claim to operate in markets which are marginally more competitive in terms of the number of competitors they faced
or their market share, and in which there was strong pressure to reduce
costs. But for the most part they endured a harsh recession, with adverse
effects upon demand, profitability and in many cases their financial viability. And this was combined with the danger and in many cases the reality
of a change in ownership status resulting from privatisation, or from

contested takeover bids. Further cases could be adduced to strengthen this argument.

However, it is important not to over-generalise. The experience of panel firms was diverse. For some the recession was mild in character and did not greatly disturb their calm and profitable oligopolistic markets. F13, for example, experienced no prolonged downturn in output. Its main difficulty was the perennial one of coping with steep fluctuations in product price: 'there is now greater competition between companies but it remains a highly profitable industry. It was never worth fighting a battle. Production had always to be maintained.' Yet for the larger group of firms, once demand conditions in the economy had recovered, there is little evidence of a marked intensification of market competition. This is congruent with the view of Millward *et al.* who found for manufacturing firms, in 1980–90, only a slight increase in the number of competitors, and that if at all, demand had become less responsive to change in price (1992: 12–13).

Employment law: company responses

The revision of employment law was initially discussed in chapter 1. Changes have been introduced to a wide range of legal provisions, including the closed shop, balloting, the liability of trade unions to damages and trade union governance and the rights of individual workers. There is a degree of consensus that changes in the framework of employment law have restricted the ability of trade unions to organise and reinforced the trend towards unilateral managerial regulation of the employment relationship. The main debate is over the significance of the role of legal reform, in relation to other changes in the economic and social structure.

Some writers have argued that the law has been of crucial significance in producing a system-wide alteration in the balance of power between management and labour. The law, it is argued, has directly affected the behaviour of industrial relations agents, causing management to become more assertive and trade unions to curtail the threat of industrial action. Layard and Nickell highlight the 'series of legislative changes' such as 'restrictions on the ability of unions to organise and on the conduct of strikes [which] have weakened unions' bargaining power. This . . . led to the defeat of the miners' strike in 1985 and the low level of industrial disputes since then' (1989: 12). Similarly, Freeman and Pelletier posit that Thatcherite industrial relations legislation 'caused much of the 1980s fall in British union density' (1990: 141).

Others have been rather more circumspect. They note that the vast majority of employers have not sought injunctive relief against trade unions for possible transgression of the law (Evans 1987, Marginson *et al.* 1988:

161). The law may have had some effect on specific sectors, such as sea transport, newspaper production and on particular types of strike activity, such as secondary action. Trades unions may have become more conscious of the sanctions, such as fines and sequestration, that may now be imposed upon them and have adapted their behaviour accordingly (Brown and Wadhwani 1990). But as Brown *et al.* (1997: 80) observe:

the legislation appears to have contributed substantially to economic performance only in the few, highly publicised cases in which extensive pre-entry closed shops and associated union controls were removed after intense conflict. Elsewhere, the key factors have been heightened product market competition and more coherent management strategy.

A number of studies of the effect of employment legislation have been conducted (Elgar and Simpson 1992, Evans 1987). The present study differs from these studies in an important respect. Labour law is complex in its constitution. The various Acts, attendant codes of practice and common law interpretations produce a disparate body of law, not easily grasped by lay persons. This study is not concerned with the detailed minutiae of the law. Others have researched this subject more comprehensively. Rather, the focus is more generally upon the role and significance of the law compared with other characteristics of the environment such as the economy. The logic in this approach is that respondents tended not to discriminate between individual provisions of the law but framed their responses as a general disposition to taking legal counsel and action.

Investigation of these competing explanations is impeded by the difficulty of isolating the products of legal reform from those that are due to economic pressures and other aspects of government policy, such as the uncompromising attitude towards industrial action in the public sector (Elgar and Simpson 1992: 2). Various questions were included on the checklist about employers' use of the law. These focused upon the effects of legal change upon management policy, the closed shop, the use of ballots, secondary action and picketing. These questions were intended less to explore the impact of the law in detail than to provide some comparison between the law and other socio-economic variables such as competition or product market recession (Elgar and Simpson 1992 is a considerably more detailed analysis).

The initial intention was to collate results for each of the questions asked. However, it is possible to present the comments more succinctly. In the main interviewees did not differentiate between the individual clauses of the law. They tended to give general answers about usage. Table 6.6 examines whether firms had attempted to apply any form of legislative remedy between 1979 and 1991. This refers mainly to applications for injunctions for infringement of the law in respect of picketing, the closed shop, indus-

Table 6.6 *Use of collective employment law 1979–1991*

	Number of firms (n = 50)
Not invoked	43
Invoked	7
Considered	21

Note:
'Considered' includes the seven firms that actually invoked legal provisions.

trial action and balloting. It also includes any other use of collective employment law or even whether use of the law has been 'considered' as a possible response. Alterations to the status of the closed shop are excluded.

Seven firms, 14 per cent of the panel, sought to invoke a provision of employment law between 1979 and 1991. Of these, five firms, 10 per cent of the panel successfully did so. The seven firms all applied for injunctive relief: four to restrain strike action and three to enforce balloting obligations. Two of the seven applications were unsuccessful. Very few firms had sought and been successful in getting legal sanctions awarded. Whether recourse to the law had been 'considered' was also assessed. Consideration might encompass taking legal counsel or preparing a report on the possible legal avenues open to management in the course of a dispute. A sizeable minority, twenty-one firms or 42 per cent of the panel, had seriously considered resorting to the law. This again is a general measure. It does not consider threats to use the law, nor are we able to examine how use of the law in 1980s compares with preceding time periods.

The consequences of legal reform may also be evaluated by looking at the readiness of employers to take recourse to the law should an opportunity arise. An attempt is made to explore this issue by making a threefold distinction. Rate '1' shows a strong preference not to go to law in any circumstance. Indicative would be comments such as 'only in the last resort' or 'our very strong preference not to'. Rate '2' indicates a preference for negotiation but a willingness to go to law if negotiation fails. Rate '3' is where the interviewee expressed no hesitation in taking recourse to law, as, for instance, 'we would not hesitate [to go to law] in any incident of illegality'. 'Usage' is again defined to include all provisions of collective employment law with the exception of the closed shop. Results are presented at Table 6.7.

Most firms claimed to be reluctant or gravely reluctant to institute legal proceedings. Only two firms said they were highly disposed to usage.

Table 6.7 *Preparedness to invoke legal proceedings*

	1	2	3
Preparedness to invoke	30	18	2

Note:
n = 50 firms.
Preparedness to invoke:
1. Strong preference not to invoke legal proceedings; only do so in extreme case.
2. Preference to resolve differences through negotiation and disputes procedure but prepared to invoke law if this fails.
3. No hesitation to invoke proceedings if law is contravened.

A third set of questions concerned interviewees' estimations of the effect of legislative change upon the employment relationship. The logic here is that management need not be greatly disposed to apply the law for it to have an effect. The law may just 'sit on their shoulder', make them feel more powerful in negotiations and in what changes they are prepared to attempt to introduce. These responses deal with power. Power is a nebulous phenomenon, dependent on action in localised contexts. People may remain ignorant of their power until they attempt to manufacture some outcome. On one level, casual statements are highly subjective and not to be trusted. But understood as such, as impressions of the impact of the law, responses can be illuminating. A threefold taxonomy has again been adopted, grounded in broad narrative distinctions. Results are shown in Table 6.8.

Despite the different approach, the large majority of interviewees again thought the law had made 'little difference' to their power in the employment relationship, or the difference was marginal compared with socio-economic factors. Less than 5 per cent of firms thought that legal reforms had significantly altered their power position in the employment relationship.

Now the accusation might be made that each of the aspects studied – use of the law, preparedness to use and assessment of agent's power – are of the law in general and that a more discriminating analysis of individual provisions, such as that for secondary action, might reveal a higher rate of usage and to greater consequence. This may be the case. But overall the law has not been employed to great effect and has had only a minimal impact directly upon managerial behaviour. Certainly, a high proportion of firms have considered recourse to the law, but few have done so, few think they

Table 6.8 *Employers' estimate of the
significance of legal reforms 1979–1991*

	1	2	3
Number of firms	35	13	2

Note:
n = 50 firms.
Impact on the employment relationship:
1. Little difference.
2. Some impact but marginal compared with
other socio-economic factors.
3. Manifestly altered the power relationship
between firm and labour.

shall do so and few think the law has materially altered their situation. This inclines towards the view expressed earlier that the law has been a significant force in certain sectors but otherwise it is a less important factor than recession or the threat of takeover because employers have not sought its application.

One bulwark for this view is provided by the case of F12, in vehicles and engineering. This firm has not invoked any aspect of the law. It 'can't foresee a situation in which it would ever use the law'. The law has made 'not a ha'pe'th of difference' to the firms' operations. Balloting is an 'added complication'. Where the law could have been applied, it has 'striven not to get involved' because 'you can't legislate for good relations'. Legal change has been important 'but not directly' because it has 'changed the environment and ambience' and forced unions 'to think'. The threat posed to union funds has allowed union leaders 'a degree of proper authority over the membership, which they had almost totally lost'. Thus the law 'has conditioned unions' rather than management's behaviour' and in this sense it has been a 'force for good'.

F4, an engineering company, said changes in the law 'had not the slightest effect'; and that no injunctions have been issued. Management prefers not to use the law and feels 'as if it has failed if it does so'. F10, a vehicle manufacturer, said there has been no pressure from company directors to use legal sanctions. They have 'not even dreamt about it': 'people tend to view it [legal sanctions] as an attack'. Another engineering conglomerate, F16, reported no use of injunctions and no attention to balloting legislation, although they do insist that unions operate within the terms of the law. The interviewee maintained that it is not possible to 'legislate' for good industrial relations, which depends upon achieving an 'appropriate' man-

agement style. Equally, F28, a publisher and printer, was reluctant to use
the law: 'we don't like giving money to lawyers.' It had not invoked any legal
proceedings. In the event where its drivers refused to deliver to a bookstore
affected by industrial action, the company preferred to 'find a way around'
the situation. Finally, F21, a chemicals company, had not been involved
with employment law – 'not a single issue'. Its trade unions had balloted
twice for industrial action, in both cases 'scrupulously' abiding by legal provisions. Instead, there was a reliance upon collective-bargaining procedures, although the personnel manager concerned suggested that
employment law changes had altered the climate of labour relations.

   Equally as common is where the firm has a strong preference not to go
to law but is prepared to in extreme circumstances. For example, F22 falls
into energy, water and chemicals. It has not applied for an injunction nor
has it threatened to do so. There have been one or two issues where the
union has acted without balloting. In these cases, the firm has drawn attention to the illegality but has been concerned mainly with the breach of procedure. But should there be a major industrial problem, the firm is
'certainly prepared to use the law'. In most cases, the unions do ballot
before taking action and it was the manager's perception that both union
and membership 'feel comfortable' with balloting. Certainly, there has been
no need to 'push unions into following the law'. F40, a food manufacturer,
said that employment law changes do 'intrude' into its industrial relations
but that one 'can't change important things by legislation'. Legal sanctions
have 'not been a major feature' and there is a strong preference not to apply
them, although the company has considered their use. Another food and
drinks firm, F43, had not applied any legal provisions but 'would not hesitate to do so if a union was transgressing the law'.

   These two categories are typical of most firms. A further example
exemplifies the third, smaller set of firms that regard the law as having been
important. F31 is in rubber, publishing and print. It has 'looked at injunctions' three or four times. The change in the law on secondary action has
been 'hugely valuable' because unions 'no longer attempt it' although the
respondent thought that if the opportunity existed 'they would do so'.
Sequestration of SOGAT's funds had a 'profound influence' and had an
'important climactic effect'. It 'altered the balance of power' because
'everyone saw the impact' and this 'concentrated their minds on prevention
rather than attack'. It also helped remove 'mavericks'. More balloting now
takes place which 'cools peoples emotions. People have more time to think
and they tend to fill the gap with more information.' Overall, 'non-use of
the law has been very valuable. The underlying message of the law has
changed to recognise the dignity of the individual. This is very healthy.' In
the oil company, F13, a union's liability for damages appears to have

'stopped situations where employees will walk out at the drop of a hat', according to our interviewee. Removing immunity for secondary action has also been important in increasing the power of ('giving more balls to') oil company management and contractors.

Employment law: employers' association responses

This section probes the attitude of employers' associations to the reform of employment law. The objective in doing so is to record the orientation of these umbrella organisations to one of the key facets of recent labour market reform.

A distinction has been drawn between use of the law and orientation towards it. Simple classes are again derived. With orientation, the response given to the question 'Do you support the reforms of employment law introduced since 1979?' were transcribed and placed into five categories, ranging from strongly disapprove, through neutrality to strongly approve. The basis for classification was key words in statements, and some of these are reproduced below to illustrate the technique. Data are displayed in Table 6.9.

Most associations on the classification 'disapproved' of the changes to employment law made under the Conservative administration. Only a small minority of associations 'approved' in broad terms and none did so strongly. Voluntarism is the streak that runs through many of the comments made. EA1, in construction and transport, is typical: 'we are opposed to the law and management have not been influenced by it. I am unaware of any injunctions.' 'Interference' was the reason cited by EA13, in food, brewing and tobacco. The law, they argue 'doesn't make for good industrial relations. It is in danger of interfering in employer/trade union affairs.' While EA6, in printing and publishing, maintained that management must rely on their internal administrative ability and not on external authority to create durable relationships: 'use of the law indicates that managers can't manage their business. In my opinion the law should not intervene. There is no justification for it.'

Comment such as this was often recorded. It expresses a preference for the state to abstain from too directly or extensively regulating the collective features of the employment relationship. Where this ethic was not deeply rooted, such as in retail, employers were more positive about legal change. But, also surprisingly, one association in textiles with a history of close co-operation with the industry union did favour legal change. They had been prepared to injunct the union during the 1984 industry-wide strike and thought balloting measures a 'good thing'. Of course, these indices cannot give anything more than a flavour of associations' attitude to the law, and

Table 6.9 *Orientation to*
employment legislation

Orientation	Number (n = 14)
Strongly approve	0
Approve	3
Neutral	3
Disapprove	7
Strongly disapprove	1

Note:
For one association, data unusable.

there is a degree of imprecision involved in categorising responses. But they are important in giving some information about a variable – legal reform – which may have been a prime stimulant of regulatory change.

Moving to use, as opposed to orientation towards, we may make a number of further remarks. Use of the law has again been calibrated on a simple, three-class scale:

1. regular: the association or a member firm had applied or threatened to apply a provision of employment law on more than five occasions;
2. occasional: applied or threatened application on three to five occasions; and
3. isolated: application or threatened application on fewer than three occasions.

This measure is subject to various possible inaccuracies. It is especially reliant on officials' accounts of their and their member firms' use or threatened use of the law. Fallible memories may intrude here. Yet, looking at Table 6.10, use of the law has been so infrequent that poor recollection is unlikely to be the main explanator. The results are quite stark. Only one association reported that it or its members had threatened to employ or had employed a provision of employment law passed by the Conservative government on more than three occasions between 1979 and 1991.

Overall, associations appear to be greatly reluctant to encourage member firms to apply legal reforms. Yet a number of caveats ought to be added. First, these aggregate findings may disguise the tendency for associations and member firms to scrutinise and draw attention to the requirements for balloting prior to industrial action, without seeking to invoke the law to correct any deficiencies. This was reported by a number of units. Furthermore the absence of the application of the law does not preclude its having had an effect. Rather like strike activity, a paucity of incidents may

Table 6.10 *Use of*
employment legislation

Use	Number is (n = 14)
Regular	0
Occasional	1
Isolated	13

Note:
For one association, data unusable.

be a sign of the law's strength rather than its irrelevance. And interviewees frequently attested to the high level of obedience by trade unions.

Advocacy of voluntarism was the main reason expressed for the limited use of employment law. Associations may adhere so closely to this creed for a number of reasons. First, the industry sectors in the panel may be structurally suited to it: small firms in textiles, knitting, clothing, with direct managerial style; consensual relations with industry trade unions; and a strong multi-employer regulatory institution. Each of these reasons tends to favour a position of non-intervention in regard to the law. There may also be a vested interest on the part of associations in retaining non-legal arrangements. The law enables firms to bypass multi-employer associations and engage in action individually.

Summary

This chapter has examined a number of environmental variables. These measures are far from sophisticated and certain subtle features of change may have escaped their net. Two of the most likely catalysts of change – competitive pressures and legislative reform – have been scrutinised. There was only a slight intensification of competition. A more significant factor was recessionary pressure, where a large share of panel firms were drastically affected by reduced profitability and a substantial proportion experienced the threat or reality of privatisation or of contested takeover bids. Few companies had taken the opportunity to apply the legislative measures of the 1980s, and few associations recommended that their members did so. Approximately half of panel companies were prepared to apply legal sanctions, if necessary.

The preference for a voluntarist approach leads to the subject of the following chapter, management industrial relations policy.

7   Management industrial relations policy

One of the key themes identified in the introduction was management industrial relations policy, which is comprised of a number of elements. Research has focused upon the extent to which personnel management orthodoxy has fragmented into a wider range of policies and styles. There are a number of elements to this debate. The first concerns personnel and industrial relations management directly, and the degree to which there has been a shift away from a 'collectivism' and towards 'individualism'. The second, related issue refers to business policies. Personnel management does not exist in a vacuum but is conditioned by broader business decisions and policies, such as the type of financial control system adopted, and the degree of corporate strategic planning. This leads on to the third issue, the degree to which employers continue to support joint regulation and a union presence. We have seen the spread of derecognition across panel firms, but have not yet commented on the extent to which management wishes to uphold union recognition in the future. The final theme for discussion is the power and the attitudes of organised labour. Management impressions of the extent to which employees are now able to resist managerial initiatives, and also workers' inclination to join and take part in union activities will be considered.

These four themes – management style, business policy, unionisation policy and the power and attitudes of labour – are examined in turn.

Management 'style'

Management style features prominently in many highly prescriptive writings on business that make reference to the management of labour. On one reading, high levels of activity might be expected for this variable. Certainly the theme has been much discussed by academics. The most frequent starting point is the taxonomy advanced by Purcell and Sisson (1983: 112–18; see also Fox 1974: 297–313). They outline five styles in the management of industrial relations. These are: traditionalist, sophisticated paternalist, sophisticated moderns (with two sub-types) and standard moderns. Two of the most important criteria that differentiate these styles are the legitimacy accorded to trade union representation and the extent to which management senses and attempts to satisfy the aspirations of employees.

Empirical studies have been unable to discern these management 'styles' with any consistency. Deaton (1985) studied WIRS for evidence of Purcell and Sisson's typology but could find no indication of coherent styles and found that many plants displayed traces of two or more styles. Edwards asked managers to provide a statement of their 'overall policy or philosophy for the management of labour relations' (1987: 135; see also Marsh 1982). Ninety per cent of managers claimed to have a policy as indicated. Classification proved difficult. An initial attempt produced fifty-five types of policy, eventually reduced to twelve by 'ignoring subtleties' and permitting 'overlap' (1987: 138). Marginson *et al.* experienced similar complications but established eleven categories by 'deducing the overall sense of a reply' (1988: 122). But they then found 'no correspondence at all' between overall descriptions and specific practice.

Management's regulation of labour administration is characterised in large measure by pragmatism and opportunism. Take, for example, F1, a manufacturer, who stated its personnel policy as: 'to achieve greenfield thinking on brownfield sites'; alternatively, F11, a vehicle manufacturer, whose mission statement is to 'achieve success through people', while F24 described its employee relations philosophy as 'to genuinely treat people better'. Equally, F22, the chemicals company, did not think of itself as 'having a strategy' and found difficult the notion of an 'overall vision' but 'at some point' would like to achieve a 'totally integrated workforce'. Finally, F31, the paper and printing firm, described its employee strategy as 'to be a good employer, to provide people at work with good conditions'.

In addition, personnel policy in 1991 was determined at site level in numerous companies. As with payment determination, identifying the authorship of a policy is complex. In several cases, companies maintained that responsibility for personnel policy had been devolved to individual site managers, but that plants were governed by a set of guiding or orienting principles. These standards were applied through a mandating process, whereby any major plant-level initiative, such as derecognition, had first to be sanctioned by headquarters. In six of the forty-three firms who commented on this specific issue, plants had unfettered discretion over personnel policy. As an example, at F7, the electronics and auto components manufacturer, personnel policy was 'unstructured' and 'completely up to site managers'. This calls into question the very use of the label 'style'. Yet even a casual inspection of the interview transcripts reveals marked

Table 7.1 *Features of contractual and normative regulation*

Feature	Contractual	Normative
Exchange	Economic	Social
Rewards	Remunerative	Group acceptance
Control	External	Internal
Obligations	Specific	Diffuse
Work role	Prescribed	Discretionary

differences in how management sought to regulate the employment relationship. These distinctions are not neatly defined (Edwards 1987: 137). Responses on the subject typically were vague and expressed as generalities, while individual policy units often seemed to be erratic and frequently to be lacking a unifying theme. But distinctions do exist nonetheless and it is possible to reveal some of these without implying a high degree of consistency or that their representation is unproblematic.

A useful starting point is the distinction made by Purcell between collectivism, 'the extent to which management policy is directed towards inhibiting or encouraging the development of collective representation by employees and allowing employees a collective voice in decision-making', and individualism, which 'refers to the extent to which personnel policies are focused on the rights and capabilities of individual workers' (1987: 533). This marries well with one of the central themes of analysis, whether collective regulation has been displaced by individual regulation.

A further component may also be introduced which is derived mainly from Fox (1974) (see also Etzioni 1961). This is to separate 'contractual', or formally specified, from 'normative', or informally specified, modes of regulation. This schema can be extended to encompass the form of the exchange transaction, rewards, work obligations and work roles (a précis is presented at Table 7.1). It parallels a distinction drawn elsewhere between market-oriented and organisation-oriented employment relations (Dore 1989, Whittaker 1990: 6–7).

The essence of contractual regulation is that the reciprocal obligations of each party are specified in detail such that the terms of exchange are clear and unambiguous. This clarity extends to the description of the work task and the form of reward. The worker does not undertake the work with the prospect of some vague future reward or as a social obligation, nor are such terms intrinsic to the exchange. Rather, reciprocal obligations are limited to those prescribed in the contract (Davis 1955: 470). The *locus* of control is a contract or set of contracts to which consenting parties refer in their assessment of correct behaviour. Terms of individual rights and obligations are codified in formal documents. In this sense 'contract' refers to all written promulgation used in the administration of labour, including employment contracts, collective agreements, job evaluation schemes, workrules and codes of behaviour and discipline.

Normative managerial regulation refers to those 'elements of the organisational value system which regulate the conduct and performance of members' (Hill 1981: 16). Exchange is based not upon specific and discrete obligations but upon a much more diffuse set of social responses, what Malinowski termed a 'configuration of obligations'. Prescribed organisational norms and values are internalised by members such that they become 'habits, skills, convictions'. Normative regulation requires of members a commitment to the work role, what Etzioni (1961) has termed 'moral commitment' or a 'position of high intensity'. The primary mode of control is self-regulation reinforced by social rewards such as expressed approval, increased social interaction and a willingness to return a favour together with social sanctions, such as the withholding of acceptance.

Contractual and normative regulation are both ideal types. Contract can never be sufficiently particularised to eliminate all ambiguity. Also, all administrative systems rely in some degree upon forms of internalised and externalised control. Still, this schema does enable us to make moderate progress. Synthesising the two elements produces three types of primary labour policy – collective-contractual, collective-normative and individual-contractual. Details of the first three are provided in Table 7.1. The fourth type, individual normative, may be of greater relevance to the work orientations of professional staff, than to the highly unionised, manual and semi-skilled groups which are the main focus in the present study. Because most firms in the panel set terms and conditions by collective bargaining in 1979, which would fall under 'collective/contractual', an examination may be made of the extent to which employers intend to move away from this mode.

Results are outlined in Table 7.2. As expected, a preponderance of firms in 1979 had a collective-contractual labour policy. They aimed to govern the employment relationship through formal contracts determined for collectivities of workers, or collective agreements. There has been a large reduction in the number of firms following this policy. Slightly less than one-quarter of firms follow a collective-normative policy, one that treats the workforce as collectivities but attempts to inculcate more co-operative attitudes. Seven firms now aim to use individual contracts, with pay and

Table 7.2 *Labour policy 1979–1991*

Number	Type	1979 (n = 50)	1991 (n = 50)
1	Collective-contractual	45	25
2	Individual-contractual	0	7
3	Collective-normative	0	11
4(i)	No central labour policy	4	6
4(ii)	No identifiable labour policy	1	1

Notes:
1. Collective-contractual: primary mode of labour regulation is a formal, written document for collectivities of workers.
2. Collective-normative: primary mode of regulation is trust-based for collectivities of workers.
3. Individual-contractual: primary mode of regulation is the individual labour contract.

conditions set by individual appraisal. This trend may be best demonstrated through a number of cases.

First, take a case where the firm has continued to follow a collective-contractual policy. This is the case at F2, in vehicles and engineering. The principal means of labour regulation is through formal agreements negotiated collectively. Pay bargaining at this firm has been decentralised but there have been few other innovations in personnel policy: 'what we can't get through collective bargaining isn't worth having.' For F11, the auto manufacturer, its long-standing collective agreement 'remains the centre of authority'. With F28, the printer and publisher, the aim is 'to achieve change through procedure': the company was 'adamant that they lay down procedure and that [managers] must follow it'. Consequently, there was a focus upon negotiating formal productivity agreements. This is quite clearly at variance with F8, in construction, transport and communications, which has ended collective bargaining and embraced individual contracts. These were introduced initially in the early 1980s for managers and subsequently for all staff:

Trade union recognition was discontinued. Grades and job evaluation schemes were removed. Pay is now determined by annual appraisal. The total budget for pay increases depends on market and profit levels. Individual managers are required to appraise staff according to a normal distribution and allocate pay rises accordingly, although there is some discretion.

Evidently, management has changed the primary mode of regulating labour. At other companies, there was a trend away from joint regulation, towards individualisation, although not to the extreme of F8, underlining the point made earlier that change is better represented as occurring along a continuum. The personnel policy of F13, an oil company, was 'not written' but a 'living thing'. It had, none the less, decisively rejected productivity bargaining (as being 'no longer productive') in favour of transferring employees to staff status, with individual contracts and pay determined by appraisal. The other oil companies, F14 and F15, had a very similar approach. In none of the oil companies had this policy been entirely implemented, with various groups of white-collar and craft employees having been transferred to individual contracts but with larger groups of manual operatives remaining covered by collective bargaining, and in certain cases having rejected individualisation through a ballot. This again can be contrasted with the instance of F39, which sought to displace a form of collectivism founded upon contractual relations with one based to a greater degree upon trust. In 1979 it fitted well into the collective-contractual division, having recently concluded a formal closed shop agreement. By 1991, it was attempting to place total quality management (TQM) at the centre of its regulatory framework. Symbolic of this is the title of 'personnel and TQM' director. An initiative of the US headquarters, TQM has been taken up 'wholeheartedly' by the UK subsidiary:

there are hundreds of project teams and voluntary improvement teams. They get together for problem-solving and make presentations to management. Teams are formed irrespective of traditional demarcation lines and each member of the workforce is sent on a four day team building course. Teamwork is now a large part of the culture and has totally changed the 'management makes change' mindset.

What management is seeking here is attitudinal change, to elicit a more positive orientation to work. They are conscious also of the benefits of this process in marginalising unions: 'the unions felt it would erode their rights but it was difficult for them to oppose.' Now it may be that these schemes are prone to break down quite rapidly, or that they are buttressed by the rather more traditional methods of direct managerial control and insistence on prerogative. But the firm could point to a series of initiatives designed to reduce their reliance on contractualised labour regulation.

Classifying labour relations policies in his way, as Edwards observes, is an 'admittedly imprecise endeavour. The overlaps between categories and the ambiguity of some of the categories themselves' are a hindrance in drawing any firm conclusions (1987: 143). Yet it has been shown that, in many firms, in 1991, management intends to move away from a collective-contractual mode of labour regulation. But there is no single model of labour policy emerging, rather a wider variety of policies appear to be being pursued. This finding has some support from other studies. Edwards maintains that the 'broad picture' of industrial relations policy in the late 1970s was 'a predominance of the negotiatory approach' (1987: 143). He suggests that the 'consultative approach' has become 'much more wide-spread' and that there is 'less reliance on negotiation with trade unions and an emphasis on dealing with the individual worker, aiming to engender a sense of commitment to company goals and to broaden the focus from wages and conditions of work' (1987: 141). We can assent to each of these points.

Business policy

The previous section examined personnel and labour relations management policy. It is necessary to contextualise labour policy by considering broader developments in business policy. Such matters are important because the approach that management takes to personnel management, for example in deciding to retain a collective contractual approach, or to shift from a 'collectivist' to an 'individualist' stance in managing the employment relationship, may be conditioned by other matters, such as the financial pressures with which managers are faced.

This section follows the method utilised in previous sections, of developing a taxonomy of policy based upon a random selection of companies, and then placing firms into this classification based upon key words and phrases used in interview. In the present section, nine categories were derived from an initial analysis of ten panel firms. These are presented in Table 7.3. As previously noted, corporate statements on business policy and objectives are typically vague. The present category reflects this. However, while managers may express their strategies in general terms, the positions they adopt may have fundamental importance to the conduct of industrial relations, a point which is illustrated below.

The names of three of the classes have been used elsewhere – 'strategic planning' and 'financial control' by Goold and Campbell (1987) and 'paternalistic' by Purcell and Ahlstrand (1993). These terms were used because there appeared to be a close correspondence between the categories created through the grounded method and those used by previous authors. It should be noted that the present study does not attempt to test the categories used elsewhere; they are merely applied as a convenient point of reference.

This codification may be open to criticism on a number of fronts. It would certainly be possible to generate far more types. It is also true that the classes are not discrete and there is overlap between some boundaries.

Table 7.3 *Categories of business policy*

Category	Business policy	Description
1	Financial control	Common financial structure across business units; close comparison of costs and profits of business units; readiness to dispose of business units which fail to meet financial targets; business units have high degree of autonomy over operational affairs.
2	Strategic planning	Extensive use of detailed, long-term strategic plans; development of an overarching corporate management philosophy and style; corporate management may intervene in operational affairs of business units to ensure consistency with corporate plan.
3	'Broad direction'	Set of principles which inform business strategy of organisation; general notion of future direction but eschews extensive strategic planning; 'simple' strategy.
4	Customer focus	High priority to relations with customers; stress customer awareness; need to be flexible to customer demands.
5	Paternalistic	Emphasis upon protection of managerial prerogative while adopting a benevolent approach to employee management; 'amateur' and 'gentlemanly' style in conducting business.
6	Market realignment	Relocate operations abroad; shed all non-core activities; move into different market sector.
7	Subcontracting	Reduce permanent workforce and employ subcontractors to reduce operating costs.
8	Re-establish managerial prerogative	Policy of capturing control of the workplace; empowering managers; extending the frontier of control.
9	Creating a 'flexible' corporate culture	Creation of 'adaptable' and 'responsive' organisation; employees who can work in a variety of roles/ tasks; 'organic' corporation.

But they are intended to reflect the styles demonstrated by panel firms. Results are presented in Table 7.4, which shows the number of firms which cited each category of business policy.

The numerically most popular business policy among panel firms, cited by twelve companies, was class 3, strategy as a 'broad direction'. For example, the personnel manager at F5, an engineering and electronics company, felt 'uncomfortable using the term "strategy"' and described the

Table 7.4 *Business policy 1979–1991*

Category	Business policy	Number of firms
1	Financial control	10
2	Strategic planning	4
3	'Broad direction'	12
4	Customer focus	9
5	Paternalistic	3
6	Market realignment	6
7	Subcontracting	5
8	Re-establish managerial prerogative	9
9	Creating a 'flexible' corporate culture	7

Note:
n = 43 firms

company as 'operators and pragmatists'. F15, an oil company, did not 'have a corporate strategy' but had instead a 'corporate direction' and a 'basic set of principles'. These were oriented towards the need to set external standards, to attract investment and to retain the company's technical edge. The chemicals company, F21, did not 'think in terms of a strategy' but of an 'overall approach'. This parallels the textiles firm, F32, which had 'no grand overall strategy' but a number of guiding principles, based around greater customer awareness, better design and continued investment.

The first category, financial control, was the second most commonly mentioned. There was evidence that this policy had become more common in the 1980s. For example, F2, an engineering company, described its 'strategic vision' as simply to achieve 'profitable growth in a variety of segments'. It is now prepared to sell businesses 'which are not making money'; in the 1970s, it did not need to take such measures. This point is echoed by F5 which had shifted to a system of stand-alone business units which it was now prepared to close down if they failed to meet profit targets. F16, an engineering conglomerate, imposes a common financial reporting structure on companies which it acquires, removing the main board and requiring chief executives to take 'tough choices' to meet the financial strictures it lays down. Its main aim is to 'get costs under control': if the 'economy dips', it 'starts to shed labour'. The building component manufacturer, F18, was acquired by a large multinational in the 1980s, which fired the previous board of directors, disposed of assets such as company housing for workers, and offered to invest in new machinery only if working practices changed.

'Customer focus' was cited as a component of business policy by nine panel firms. For example, F25, a transport company, had attempted to shift from a 'producer' to a 'customer' orientation, seeking to market a number of 'business brands'. F32, a textiles manufacturer, aimed to 'respond more quickly to customers', and for 'closer relations between customers and employees at all levels of the business'. Category 8, 're-establish managerial prerogative', was also mentioned by nine firms. For instance, F41, a tobacco company, had brought in 'hard men' to 'drive change through', while F27, a printer and publisher aimed to change the managerial culture: 'to sew the balls back on to our managers', as our interviewee put it.

The ninth class, 'creating a flexible organisation culture', was mentioned by seven firms. As an illustration, F43 described its business policy as creating a 'fast, responsive' organisation, in which the 'competitive edge is the organisation itself', an organisation which is 'open to any kind of alliance'. The 'overall approach' is the 'summation of trends in Rosabeth Moss Kanter's book [*The Change Masters*, 1984]'. F30, an electronics manufacturer, aimed to create a 'mindset' of a company 'capable of achieving anything', while at F40, a food manufacturer, the business was seen as a 'learning organisation', in which 'quality and learning initiatives are for real'.

Five firms mentioned 'market realignment'. For example, F5 had a policy of selling its UK manufacturing operations and opening overseas plants, while also shifting its focus from manufacturing batteries to the electronics sector. Other companies were internationalising, rather than simply relocating. F20, a consumer products manufacturer, was becoming more international in its operations, by making strategic purchases of businesses in markets which it wished to develop, and integrating such acquisitions within its systems of governance and administration.

'Subcontracting' was a theme raised by five companies, notably those in the oil and automotive sectors. F14 explained that volatile oil prices had made long-term investment policies more problematic, so the company had shifted to a greater dependence upon contractors as a means of reducing costs and managing peaks and troughs of product demand. The construction company, F19, had also turned towards contracting as a means of lowering costs and raising quality.

The 'strategic planning' class was mentioned by four firms. F20, for instance, a consumer goods manufacturer conducts 'much planning for the future' including annual and five-year plans, stating that it needs a 'comprehensive view of [its] requirements'. F37, a retailer and distributor, maintained that it was 'textbook' in its business policy, having a one-year operational and a five-year strategic plan. F23, a utility, engaged in a major strategic review in the early 1980s. It decided it was 'status conscious and not cost conscious' and that 'we lacked a customer focus'. All committees that ran the firm were dismantled. A mission statement was written with strong personnel policy objectives:

We set up a management development committee on which the chief executive spent 20 per cent of his time. We instituted a major review of staff. The top five hundred managers underwent psychometric appraisal and their careers were evaluated on this basis. Many left as a result. Training programs for those remaining were designed from the appraisal data. All subsequent promotion required experience in a function that was not the manager's speciality.

Finally, three firms included a 'paternalistic' approach in their description of business policy. Table 7.5 presents the data on business policy by industry sector. There appears to be a concentration of firms citing a financial control policy in sector 2 (vehicles and heavy engineering). In sector 1 (energy and chemicals), there is a small cluster of firms with 'subcontracting', reflecting the presence of the oil companies in this sector and their tendency to pursue similar policies. In addition, sector 6, which includes retail distribution, has three companies which included 'customer focus' within their statements on business policy, which reflects the dynamics of this sector. Otherwise, the absence of a strong sectoral pattern is notable, with each of the six industry sectors containing a wide range of orientations.

Tables 7.3 to 7.5 separated out elements of policy, for ease of presentation and analysis. If the business policies of individual companies are examined, at least as expressed within our interviews, what comes across most strongly is the wide array of methods and approaches – their eclecticism (Marginson et al. 1994). Take, for example, F4, the engineering company, which combines elements of 'financial control' by stressing that 'accountants run the company', with an admittedly 'paternalistic' approach to its employees, and a 'liking for rules and regulations' and a 'continuity of style'. F40, a food manufacturer, is similarly disparate in its business policy, emphasising its 'strong paternalistic tradition' and also that 'HRM and TQM have been embraced by the whole board'. In other cases, though, there is a more easily discernible pattern to business policy. F36, a retailer, aimed to compete with the 'upmarket' supermarkets, which was consistent with its installation of new 'sales based ordering' technology, and its 'customer first' employee-training programme. With F28, a publisher, a similar thread could be traced, which ran from the declining margins of book publishing, to a focus upon overhead costs and staff reductions, which in turn led to 60 per cent of staff being made redundant and replaced by freelance contractors.

Table 7.5 *Business policy 1979–1991, by sector*

Category	1 Energy, minerals, chemicals	2 Vehicles, shipbuilding, engineering	3 Food, brewing, tobacco	4 Rubber, Plastics, print	5 Construction, transport, communications	6 Distribution: retail, wholesale, film
1 Financial control	1	5	1	1	1	1
2 Strategic planning	1	0	1	1	0	1
3 'Broad direction'	3	3	1	2	1	2
4 Customer focus	1	1	2	2	0	3
5 Paternalistic	1	1	1	0	0	0
6 Market realignment	0	1	1	2	1	1
7 Subcontracting	3	1	0	0	1	0
8 Re-establish managerial prerogative	0	1	3	2	0	1
9 Creating a 'flexible' corporate culture	1	2	2	2	1	1

Note:
n = 43 firms

Table 7.6 *Unionisation policy 1979–1991*

Number	Type	1979 (n = 50)	1991 (n = 50)
1	Active support	9	7
2	Preference	25	15
3	Indifferent	10	9
4	Reduction	4	18
5	No identifiable union policy	2	1

Unionisation policy

The survey of management style and labour policy has thus far been limited to the broad direction of content. This section looks more closely at the attitude of companies towards unionisation. It is especially important to do so because much of the expanding influence of trade unions at the time of the 1979 study, through the granting of facilities to shop stewards, the formalisation of bargaining procedures and so on, derived ultimately from a managerial decision to support the extension of joint determination. Whether this support continues to distinguish sample firms needs to be subjected to scrutiny.

Based on the narrative comments of respondents, a simple scale has been constructed. This separates those firms where no identifiable union policy could be discerned from those where a policy, however broad, was articulated. With the latter, four points were differentiated.

1. active support for unionisation; that is, where the company would consistently assist the union in its attempts to recruit, such as by including a union membership form in the job application form, or by allowing stewards to address or talk individually to new recruits;
2. where the firm 'prefers' strong membership but would not take steps to encourage workers to join;
3. where the company is indifferent to the level of unionisation; and
4. where the firm is seeking to reduce the extent of union influence, such as encouraging workers to vote for derecognition or deliberately transferring production to non-union sites.

Data are at Table 7.6.

It is worth remembering that these figures refer not to what has happened but to what, at that point in time, the firm is trying to bring about. Given this qualification, a number of points can be made. First, on the above definition, only a minority of companies ever actively sought to encourage union membership. However in 1979, half of panel firms had a preference for strong union organisation, while only a small minority, four firms, had been seeking to reduce the extent of unionisation. There had by 1991 been a considerable reversal in these policies. Almost one-third of firms now state that their policy preference is to diminish the extent of unionisation. There had been a reduction by almost half in the proportion of firms preferring strong unions, although the fall in the number actively supporting unionisation was not nearly so pronounced.

In 1979, over two-thirds of companies 'preferred' or 'actively supported' unionisation; by 1991, the majority were indifferent or were seeking to undermine the role of unions. A fitting example of this trend is F15. This company in 1979 had been deliberately sponsoring trade unionism through the formalisation of bargaining agreements and other measures in line with the recommendations of the Donovan report. It had multiple union representation. By 1991, it had embarked on a policy of 'systematically reducing the pillars of union power', to derecognise and 'reduce the number of unions': 'we want to change the environment to single union or non-union, to have simpler structures.' F1, an engineering company with multiple union recognition, described itself as 'neutral towards unions but would like to derecognize'. F3, a manufacturer of cables, had a policy of negotiating formal post-entry closed shops in 1979, but by 1991 was 'prepared to derecognise', if necessary. F8, a telecommunications and manufacturing company, argued that derecognition 'sits more comfortably' with its business policy.

The second most populous group had a 'preference' for union membership but would not actively support it. F32, a textiles manufacturer, said it 'encouraged union membership' and was not 'tempted to derecognise'. A retailer and manufacturer, F34, said it too 'encouraged union membership' and 'won't derecognise, other than in exceptional cases'. The category which included those 'indifferent' to union membership amounted to nine firms in 1991. For example, F33, a retailer with highly unionised warehouse and distribution facilities, had a policy in 1979 of neutrality towards unions, although it would accept the closed shop 'where it exists'. By 1991, its neutrality towards unions had hardened, describing its policy as 'distant, formal and correct' towards unions, with derecognition 'not beyond the pale'. F9, the metal manufacturer, was 'tolerant' in 1979 of the closed shop but by 1991 its policy was to 'neither encourage, nor discourage' union membership.

A small minority, seven firms, professed 'active support' for union membership. F19, for instance, a construction company, declared its 'belief in strong unions', while F20, a consumer products manufacturer, would 'rather deal with strong rather than weak unions'. Where membership levels fall, the company will draw this to the attention of the appropriate union official.

Labour

The question of whether management felt that they became more powerful in relation to labour in the 1980s, and whether the attitude of workers towards union membership altered is now raised. The survey examined at length management's thoughts and opinions about trade unions and the workforce. This material is highly impressionistic and difficult to substantiate in the secondary data. The study is concentrated at two points where opinions and beliefs may be examined with some validity.

The first of the two issues is respondents' impressions of the management–labour power relationship in the 1980s. The largest bargaining unit in terms of employment was examined. These are most likely to be manual and therefore better organised groups. Power, as we have stated earlier, is a nebulous phenomenon, one manifested in highly localised events and relationships. To talk in terms of power resources at a general level can be quite misleading. But there is more justification for discussing the impression of agents about their freedom to act, their fear of disruption by other parties, the countenance given to threats of strike action, for example. These were classed on the basis of key words and statements into a threefold scale: little perceived shift in the labour relationship; increased though not complete managerial power; and, finally, a total collapse of labour power. Further details of the scale are displayed in Table 7.7. The most efficacious way to illustrate the method adopted is *via* the two cases presented at the close of the section.

These data suggest quite simple findings. The first may be observed in Table 7.7, which is concerned with the management–labour power relationship. Managers overwhelmingly thought themselves to be more powerful than twelve years ago, that they had greater freedom to act and were faced with fewer disruptions or threats of strike action. In about one-quarter of cases they felt that labour power had fallen to the point where they had absolute discretion to organise work and had not been presented with realistic threats of industrial unrest. On the basis of their own responses at least, managers conceived themselves to be more powerful at the end than at the start of the 1980s. This finding also comes across strongly in the narratives of interviewees.

A related issue is the orientation of workers towards collective organisation. Here an examination was made of managers' comments on the attitudes and beliefs of the workforce, and whether workers had become less receptive to unionisation. Fresh employer policies and changes in

Table 7.7 *Perceptions of the management–labour power relationship 1979–1991*

Number	Type	1979–91 (n = 50)
1	Little alteration	5
2	Managerial power enhanced	32
3	Managerial power greatly enhanced	13

Notes:
1. Little alteration.
2. There are still constraints on management's freedom to organise work and industrial disruption continues to be threatened but with less frequency than in 1979.
3. Constraints on management's freedom to organise work have fallen to the point of being completely absent. Union power has fallen to the extent that threats of industrial action can no longer realistically be made.

employment law may have led workers to become less well disposed towards union membership.

The method employed is similar to that used to examine labour power. The subject of analysis is the largest bargaining unit. This point needs to be underlined because the largest bargaining units were most often manual groups, and it is white-collar workers who in previous sections have shown the greatest predilection for exiting union membership. Key words and statements from managers have been placed on a four-point scale, running from 'strong loyalty', to 'weakened attachment', through to 'indifference' and then positive 'hostility'. The assumption is that in 1979 workers were strongly attached to union membership. The basis of the enquiry is not rates of membership but opinions about the desirability of membership, about whether workers feel morally obliged to join. In two-thirds of the panel, respondents' comments could best be classed as indicating a 'strong loyalty' (Table 7.8). In about one-quarter of firms there had been some weakening of attachment and in only a very small minority did workers express indifference or hostility towards union membership.

The foregoing scrutiny of power and orientation is rather brief. But it is founded on strong statements made in interview and, to catch some of the atmosphere of the charges made, it is best to present some cases. A first is the atypical case, where labour power has been greatly reduced and the orientation of workers to collective organisation, it is asserted, has changed. This is F27, in division 4 (print and publishing). In 1979, labour

Table 7.8 *Orientation of labour towards*
trade union organisation 1979–1991

Number	Type	1979–91 (n = 50)
1	Strong loyalty	32
2	Weakened attachment	12
3	Indifference	5
4	Hostility	1

was powerfully organised. The ethic of unionisation was embedded. The firm had centralised negotiations and its personnel structure in an attempt to control labour disruption. Since then, union organisation has fallen into 'total disarray'. The NUJ has 'suffered enormously' and its membership level has considerably fallen. It has been derecognised in some plants and 'nobody can see any reason to join'. The attitude of workers towards the union altered because it has performed so poorly.

At F31, a paper and printing firm, there has been a 'huge reduction in union strength', with the unions 'going through a rough time due to reduced membership numbers and income'. Technological change has been important in undermining union power, since the NGA can no longer argue that 'new machinery is difficult to operate'.

More reflective of developments is F41, in division 3 (food, brewing and tobacco). In 1979 this firm reported a powerful union network and high levels of worker loyalty. The stewards were 'dominant'. They were responsible for communication on the shopfloor, and if 'people had a problem, they went to the stewards'. In the 1970s:

we had to cosset the convenors, to take them out to dinner. We didn't manage the company as such, we had to get things done as a favour.

The power context has since altered. The trade unions have 'lost power'. Managers 'don't feel hidebound by trade unions any more'. The full-time convenor has gone and 'management is not frightened anymore'. But the core attitudes of the workforce and the stewards have not been swayed. The stewards still regard team briefings as propaganda. Union pressure is 'still latent, there is still life in the union yet', and some negotiations have been on the brink of dispute.

Similarly, at F2, a multi-divisional engineering firm, the unions in 1979 'threatened to bring out the entire group if we closed one plant down'. Now, the union members are 'no longer confident that the union can keep their job', and there have been 'no examples where the unions have stood in the way of change programmes'. At F5, the union have 'given up their aspirations [to control] job territories'. The auto manufacturer, F12, said that the unions 'became weaker' in the 1980s, partly because they believed management's information about the threat of Japanese competition, whereas previously they would have dismissed such messages as propaganda. For the chemicals company, F21, many union demands in the 1970s were claims for additional rights, with management 'on the defensive'. In the 1980s, by contrast, the fall in union membership 'probably weakened the unions', union officials have 'largely accepted the change in power' and shop stewards are 'less dominant'. The outcome is that management 'can now launch in initiative with a reasonable chance of success', as the auto manufacturer, F11, put it.

The weakening of union power has been accompanied by a change in a union's bargaining stance. The personnel manager at F40, the food manufacturer, recalled that in 1979 the TGWU engaged in 'mindless power bargaining' and TGWU shop stewards were 'very confrontational' and they seemed 'to routinely oppose' management. More co-operative relations appear to have prevailed, at certain companies. F1 described the engineering unions as 'more co-operative', with the AEU prepared to 'enter into partnership'. At F5, there was 'greater co-operation' from the unions – 'as much flexibility as we can use'. The metal manufacturer, F9, found that the 'idea of "perpetual confrontation" has disappeared', and that unions are now 'knowledgeable and committed'.

Union bargaining power has not been extinguished but remains dormant, for the majority of companies. At F11, an auto manufacturer, there is no 'overt politicising' among union organisers, as there was in the 1970s. It is no longer a case of employees automatically saying that they 'can't do it' and a 'strike is no longer their first thought'. It is, our interviewee maintained, not that shop stewards' principles have changed ('not a case of grey haired stewards seeing the light') but that they operate in a different environment.

Summary

Perhaps of all the chapters, this can be said to have displayed the greatest degree of change. There has been a sizeable shift in management style from collective- contractual to individualised policies and ones based upon trust. Such changes are reinforced by broader business policies, with the most frequent approaches emphasising financial control, customer focus, and re-establishing management control. While there has been a sheer decline in the proportion of firms who are supportive of unionisation and a quite large increase in those that would like to see union representation reduced. The large majority of managers thought that their power in relation to organised labour had been enhanced in the 1980s. Only a minority of respondents were of the opinion that the relationship between workers and their unions had been weakened.

8   Discussion

The introduction argued that the economic crisis of the early 1980s was characterised by a sharp recession and an intensification of competitive pressures on a global scale. The crisis was particularly severe in Britain, which experienced a steep downturn in product market demand. There was also a far-reaching overhaul of employment law, which was intended, in part at least, to undermine trade union organisation and to limit the threat of industrial action posed by unions. These changes, taken together, had the effect of increasing managerial prerogative on the shopfloor, and stimulating the reform of workrules and practices. The vehicle for much change was negotiated agreement through formal collective-bargaining procedures. But there was also evidence of a greater diversity in management policy in the 1980s. The Donovan model of formalised, decentralised joint regulation appeared to be giving way to a greater range of management policies and styles.

The 'strategic choice' studies of Kochan *et al.* (1986) had perhaps gone furthest in proposing an integrated theory of how economic pressures may give rise to a plurality of management policy responses, and a resulting variation in the extent and pattern of workrule reform between firms in any one sector. But the principal weakness of these studies was their failure to show how strategic choice, and especially management choice, was exercised in action. Other studies proved to be rather more elaborate, illustrating that product market signals may be ambiguous and subject to interpretation by management, how management's sensing of external cues is informed by their cognitive schema, together with the culture and structure of the organisation within which the decision was taken.

In this final chapter, the principal findings of the study are first summarised, and then followed by a broader discussion of competitive pressures and industrial relations change as it applied to panel firms.

Patterns of institutional and workrule change

These data have charted an intricate mosaic of change and continuity in work relations. One of the key findings of the study was the diversity of rates of change among the various industrial and occupational groups. With manual and craft groups, evidence was found that collective organisation remained strong throughout the duration of the study. Most firms continued to bargain collectively for the largest group of workers, predominantly manuals. Little decline was evident in the rates of craft and blue-collar union density. The closed shop for manual workers had generally survived but frequently as an informal, often unwritten arrangement that the parties were sometimes reluctant to acknowledge. For white-collar workers, by contrast, considerable erosion in collective organisation was apparent. Slightly above half of employees in non-manual groups remained members of trade unions. But trade union membership was substantially lower than it had been in 1979. A much greater incidence of derecognition was recorded among white-collar workers, which was attributed primarily to the sharp fall in union density rates within this group. Equally, for non-manuals, the presence of the closed shop had receded to the point where it was barely registered.

It is important not to over-emphasise the security of collective organisation in panel firms. In a number of cases, despite a long-standing history of cohesive union organisation, and the concerted attempts of management and trade unions to support it, the closed shop was terminally weakened by the outflow from union membership. A small number of companies had actively sought to discontinue collective bargaining. Even where joint institutions remained in place, widespread decentralisation of pay bargaining was noted, although corporate centres claimed to have retained some degree of control, either directly or informally, over what rates of pay were set at establishment level. There was also a marked fall in the rate of membership of employers' associations. Many companies perceived their departure from multi-employer bodies and industry-wide bargaining as an opportunity to restructure and, where necessary, withdraw internal collective bargaining arrangements.

This pattern of change and continuity was the outcome of a complex combination of events. A variable of primary importance was the ability of trade unions to organise and bargain on behalf of their membership, with non-manual unions perceived to be considerably less effective than their manual counterparts. An additional variable was the relative indifference of the bulk of managers interviewed to the issue of union recognition and even of the closed shop. In the large majority of cases, management expressed no strong opinions about the closed shop and were prepared, as Dunn and Wright (1993) observed, 'to let sleeping dogs lie'. Where management did express a view about the closed shop it was most commonly in terms of support for the practice, citing long-standing arguments in favour of the need for workplace order and in preference for well-organised union representation.

Quite why management remained sanguine about trade union representation and the closed shop is more difficult to explain. Management may have been able to achieve the changes they wanted, such as the reform of work practices, by negotiating through existing procedures. Equally, the introduction of new systems of employee communications, such as team briefing for example, may not have required negotiation and been simply imposed by management. In both cases, management may have had no incentive to disturb long-standing instruments of employee representation. But this also implies that collective organisation was not as potent a force in 1991 as it had been in 1979. This point is consistent with interviewees' sense of having more power in collective bargaining negotiations, and being better able to secure their bargaining preferences. It is also reinforces similar findings by Morris and Wood (1991), Storey (1992), Gregg and Yates (1991) and others.

It is also important to acknowledge that, even where it survived, the constitution of the closed shop had frequently been substantially altered. At the start of the study, the closed shop for manual and non-manual employees was most frequently a formal arrangement, explicitly agreed between management and union officials. By 1991, compulsory unionism was, to a much greater degree, sustained by informal support from management, and by tacit, covert practices among workgroup members. In this sense, the closed shop lacked legitimacy, in that it did not derive from an explicit, legally sanctioned agreement. This mode of organisation, it might be argued, is potentially more fragile, and more easily undermined by the actions of management. This pattern reflects the work orientations of manual and craft groups who, for the most part, continue to command the 'strong loyalty' of the workforce.

On substantive workrules, considerable evidence was found of the widespread reform of work organisation. Examples of changes to production standards, job controls and work structuring were cited. But the degree of reform appeared to vary substantially, with some companies having systematically overhauled working practices, while others had achieved only limited change.

While only a minority of firms had withdrawn collective bargaining rights for some occupational groups, support for union representation and joint regulation in panel companies was weakening. A majority of firms continued to uphold collective bargaining as a means of setting the terms and conditions of employment, and to support or be indifferent towards union membership within their organisation. Equally, only limited evidence was found of detailed strategic planning of labour relations. But a growing minority stated that their future policy entailed the individualisation of the employment relationship, or an expansion in the sphere of unilateral managerial workrules. Consonant with this was a growth in the share of employers aiming to reduce the presence of unions within their firms.

At the level of the employers' association, there was evidence of considerable reorganisation. One third of associations had changed their names, commonly reflecting their recomposition as trade associations, rather than employers' associations. The bulk of associations' work remained in the sphere of negotiating collective agreements, representing their industry's interests to government and offering advice on employment law. There was some expansion in associations' provision of consultancy to their member firms. The coverage of industry agreements had contracted, commonly due to the withdrawal of large firms which no longer wished to be tied to common industry pay rates. Consistent with the findings for companies, employers' associations indicated that manual union organisation remained largely robust, that there had been limited derecognition and that they largely retained a voluntarist stance on employment law.

To summarise, the study reveals an intricate and multi-faceted pattern of evolution in the institutions and conduct of industrial relations. A melange of continuity and change was observed, the degree of which varied according to the occupational group, the bargaining issue and the formality of the practice under consideration. For manual and craft groups, and for core bargaining issues such as union recognition and union density, a notable degree of continuity was registered. But the level of payment determination and the form of the closed shop altered substantially. While the majority of companies continued to adhere to a policy of joint regulation, support for alternative approaches based upon management unilateralism was growing. Among non-manual groups, the erosion of collective bargaining institutions was much more substantial. The analysis of work practices suggested that, while a degree of reform was common to most panel firms, considerable diversity was noted in the extent to which firms had implemented change.

The objective of the remainder of this chapter is to examine in greater detail why the pattern of workrule change appears to have been so variable. We shall show how a broadly common competitive shock created various trajectories of procedural and substantive rule reform. These developments are then considered in the light of the model of 'strategic choice' outlined in chapter 1.

Competitive crisis, managerial frames of reference and the reform of workrules

The introduction noted several defining characteristics of an economic crisis. The first was the element of compulsion, in that firms may be faced with extreme pressures to reform long-standing methods of operation. In evolutionary economics, for example, it is assumed that change is 'problem-driven', with rapid reform of ingrained practices being impelled largely by external pressures such as an intense competitive threat. In strategic management, too, external market forces may build to the point where an 'action threshold' is reached, or where there exists a 'perceived imbalance', such that the possible costs of a failure to take action become too great to bear. A second trait of an economic crisis is the increase in levels of uncertainty. Crisis conditions are typically qualitatively different to those that preceded them, so that there may be a rupturing of expectations, and a sense that the future is less predictable. Economic crisis may also throw up unique or complex problems, for which there is no reliable method for problem formulation or analysis.

The economic environment issues a profusion of information signals and cues, which may be indistinct and rapidly changing and must be construed against a backdrop of high uncertainty. Management's reading of these signals, it was argued, is 'filtered' by their frame of reference. This schema was defined as a 'knowledge system' and 'set of expectations' which guides managerial interpretation, inference and action (Boland *et al.* 1990). Frames of reference may vary widely among managers within a single industry (Reger 1990), and due to the differing background, education and personality characteristics of individuals. But managers within any single enterprise may develop elements of the cognitive schema which they hold in common – what Prahalad and Bettis (1986) refer to as a 'dominant managerial logic'. Managerial frames of reference may also incorporate assumptions about the scope for action, or the feasibility of resolving a problem. While there may be 'objective' limitations upon action, such as scarce resources, as Weick (1979) observes, barriers may also be presumed to exist on the basis of collective avoidance of tests.

The introduction further maintained that managers may be inclined to accept the validity of signals which are consistent with their frames of reference, and discount or ignore others which are inconsistent with such belief systems. This assumes of course, that management are not fully informed about their environment. Rather, in line with behavioural economists, it is assumed that managers possess partial information about their environment, that in a crisis situation such information is ambiguous and may be of doubtful provenance, and that there are limits upon the information gathering and processing ability of individual managers – what Cyert and March (1992) termed 'bounded rationality'. Consequently, economic cues are unlikely to give rise to a uniform pattern of response from firms within any industry sector but are 'refracted' through different frames of reference and decision styles to produce varying interpretations of the initial event. The outcome, as was noted in chapter 1, may be a wide range of reactions to a competitive threat, which range from avoidance of acknowledging that a change in the environment has taken place, to a partial adaptation to the new conditions, and to decisive or transformational change.

How far does such a scenario apply to the present panel of firms? Certainly, there was an element of compulsion in the recessionary pressure of the early 1980s. Chapter 7 showed that many firms experienced a sharp downturn in product market demand in the early 1980s. Comments such as 'especially severe', and 'desperate state of the industry' were frequently recorded. Several firms faced the possibility of bankruptcy. This downturn was temporary, and many firms returned to profitability in the middle and late 1980s. But there was also some intensification of product market and of capital market pressures. Chapter 7 showed that 40 per cent of panel firms underwent a forced change in ownership, in the form of privatisation or a contested stock market takeover.

These conditions forced an initial wave of restructuring. Firms were compelled to take measures to ensure their continued viability. Action was initially largely confined to short-term cost-reduction measures. The outcome in the short term was a comparatively similar pattern of wage freezes, labour shedding and changes to work practices within panel firms. Chapter 4 showed that most firms could point to some examples of change to staffing levels or job controls. Job shedding and plant closures would also have been widespread.

It is also reasonable to assume that the effect of the rapid swing between severe recession and partial recovery was to make the external environment of the 1980s more uncertain. We noted in the introduction that for much of the post-war period, panel firms had traded in relatively stable and ordered product markets, in which demand was buoyant. At the start of the study in 1979, many companies were operating on the assumption that competitive conditions would remain favourable and their future would be relatively secure. The competitive shocks of the early 1980s disrupted long-standing trends and confounded future expectations. Between 1979 and 1982, the labour market also underwent profound upheaval. Interviewees in 1979 generally foresaw a continued expansion in the coverage of collective bargaining and the closed shop. Few anticipated the progressive changes to trade union law, nor the defeat of powerful industrial groups, such as the miners and printers, which occurred in the 1980s. Finally, a multiplicity of ostensibly new management systems, including 'Japanese management' and 'hard' and 'soft' HRM, were formulated and propounded in the 1980s. These systems were often presented as alternatives to the orthodoxy of joint regulation in union firms.

Thus panel firms had to contend with environmental pressures to change working practices, together with greater uncertainty over the future development of product markets and labour markets. The significance of these shifts had to be interpreted by management. It was not only the external environment that had to be sensed by management but also internal conditions, especially relations with labour. Changes in employment law and in the labour market did not automatically translate into greater managerial power on the shopfloor. Much depended upon the context of localised power relationships, including the strength of union organisation, the ability of management negotiators, and the vulnerability to closure of the establishment in question. Management's scope to introduce changes to working practices was not predetermined or necessarily clear-cut but was contingent upon their perception of the state of the bargaining relationship at the workplace.

In summary, managers in panel firms received a dual set of information signals in the 1980s, one from the external product and labour market context, which had to be interpreted in terms of their meaning for the firm under question, and a second set of signals from the firm's plants and establishments, such as the scope to change working practices, and the degree of labour resistance that might be encountered to change management initiatives (Figure 8.1). We noted above that managerial frames of reference inform their reading of external cues, and the following section discusses this issue in detail.

Uncertainty and managerial frames of reference

The external environment of the 1980s was characterised by crisis and a heightened sense of uncertainty. Under conditions such as these, the decisions of senior management may reflect their deep rooted systems of value and belief (Storey and Sisson 1993). The 'management policy group', the dominant elite or network of individuals responsible for the formation of policy on employment relations matters and for allocating resources, therefore becomes the focus for analysis. The boundaries of policy-making groups are normally open and fluid. They might encompass board directors, senior managers and trade union representatives. The purpose of the concept is 'primarily to distinguish between those who normally have the power to take the initiative on matters such as the design of the organisation structure from those who are in a position of having to respond to such decisions' (Child 1972: 14).

Policy group members construct an interpretative schema through which events are perceived and meanings imputed to them (Weick 1979: 156). This conceptual framework is comprised of beliefs and assumptions that are generally accepted to be valid. The schema provides a cognitive map, or ingrained pattern of thought, through which decision-problems are 'filtered'. The myths, symbols, rituals and language of group members are 'sedimented' within their frame of reference. Latent norms and values may be barely perceived at the conscious level and rarely subject to close scrutiny by group members (Janis 1982: 257). Members may create a selective bias in how they respond to factual information and to judgements from outside critics.

Power differentials may reinforce this tendency towards 'groupthink', by creating a vested interest in the obedience and conformity of less dominant members (Janis 1982). A challenge to the stereotypes, illusions or commitments of the group may be characterised as deviant behaviour, which may result in punishment through isolation or rejection. Such pressure may interfere with critical thinking, as members' striving for acceptance overrides their motivation to realistically appraise alternative courses of action. Members may minimise the importance of their doubts and assure themselves that their misgivings are erroneous and too unimportant to be worth mentioning (Janis 1982: 258). Their dependency upon the group leader for status and self-esteem may strengthen the tendency for self-censorship.

The frame of reference of the policy group may define the 'width of agenda', the range of options that are defined for the purposes of making a decision (Loasby 1976: 79). A relatively closed 'loop' of defined expectations, delimited boundaries of possibility and fixed menus of choice may be produced. For example, in the recession of 1980–2, a tyre manufacturer implemented a series of cost-cutting measures but left work organisation essentially unchanged. Once the product market recovered, the firm commissioned a management consultancy to evaluate efficiency levels within the firm. This happened largely by chance, as senior managers were opposed to employing outside consultants, but one such firm offered to work on a payment-by-costs-saved basis. Management placed the consultants in their most modern and efficient plant, with the expectation that no major efficiency gains could be made. The consultants refused to negotiate change with trade unions. They kept output constant and halved the workforce. Job tasks were re-timed at an accelerated rate and the least productive workers were made redundant.

Neither the higher production frontier nor the flat refusal to negotiate change was considered feasible by management prior to the consultants' exercise. It was henceforth adopted as standard at all sites. Product market conditions alone were insufficient to compel the firm to adopt the new standard of operating efficiency; this had to be vividly demonstrated before it could be grasped by management. Policy groups may be insensitive to opportunities for learning which require that they confront the limitations of their existing conceptual apparatus, and which may have negative and painful associations. Groups may instead be content to 'satisfice' within the boundaries of their existing cognitive framework. This is not to suggest that environmental pressures cannot induce a change in management behaviour. It is to claim that external pressures do not of themselves restructure, indeed may be congruent with, the long-term beliefs and values of group members.

Of course, these value systems are not static but are constantly evolving and interacting with a variety of stimuli. Any social group will be characterised by a variety of viewpoints, and the dominant viewpoint may be contested. Policy group powers are constrained by internal organisational control systems, and by the external environment. But these interactions will be contextualised by core frames of reference, which may be relatively impervious to competitive shocks.

Policy groups may be distinguished in the orientation of their frames of reference, which may be classified according to a number of criteria (Table 8.1). The first is the interpretation of product market signals. Policy groups had some freedom to assess information cues, and to accept, ignore, suppress or dismiss them. Certain groups tended to avoid acknowledging the implications of market signals, while others were focused to a greater degree upon short-term and long-term product market trends. The second criterion is the orientation towards labour management policy techniques. Certain groups strongly preferred to retain extant collective bargaining institutions, and to negotiate change through productivity agreements and were suspicious or dismissive of HRM initiatives. Other groups were much more inclined to innovate, and to adopt HRM practices alongside, or in place of bargaining procedures.

The third criterion is the room for manoeuvre, or scope for reforming workrules, as perceived by management. Certain groups foresaw a narrow range of opportunities for reform, while others were much more optimistic. The fourth variable is change-management style. In certain cases, this was routinely characterised by poor planning and co-ordination. Other groups focused upon securing the consent of employees, or of union groups, while others were much more uncompromising, and were willing to risk labour resistance in order to implement desired changes. Related to change-management style was the fifth criterion, the time horizon of the group. This ranged from short-term crisis management, to a focus upon short-term profit maximisation, through to a longer-term emphasis upon market share and sectoral dominance. The sixth and final criterion was the nature and extent of workrule reform. As was seen in chapters 2, 3, 4 and 5, firms varied widely in the degree to which they had changed procedural and substantive workrules.

Table 8.1 *Managerial frames of reference*

	Inert	Conservative proceduralist	Conservative innovators	Aggressive proceduralist	Radical innovators
Product market signals	Dismissive of change until crisis occurs	Attuned to long-term market trends	Attuned to long-term market trends	React to short-term market trends	React to short-term market trends
Orientation to HRM techniques	Limited awareness	Suspicious	'Soft' HRM	Suspicious	'Hard' HRM
Orientation to collective bargaining	Reliance upon established institutions	Strong preference	Retain	Strong preference	Derecognise
Perception of bargaining relationship	Narrow scope for change	Moderate scope for change	Moderate scope for change	Wide scope for change	Wide scope for change
Change-management style	Poor planning and co-ordination	Risk averse – union endorsement	Risk averse – employee consent	Risk-bearing – uncompromising	Risk-bearing – uncompromising
Time horizon	Measures sufficient to offset crisis	Long-term market share	Long-term market share	Short-term profit maximisation	Short-term profit maximisation
Workrule change	Limited changes	Incremental substantive rule change	Incremental procedural and substantive change	Substantive rule change – extent unpredictable	Procedural and substantive rule change – extent unpredictable

From the above criteria, five generic types of policy group may be differentiated.

Inert

'Inert' groups tended to dismiss product market signals as irrelevant until a crisis developed and action was undeniably required. This group was, perhaps, more complacent about, or resigned to, its standing in the product market. They tended to ignore signals with negative connotations, such as the need to raise rates of productive efficiency, until the situation could no longer be avoided. These groups demonstrated a low level of awareness of HRM techniques and relied upon established institutions by default. Proposals to challenge entrenched practices were often dismissed as unrealistic. Group members may have colluded to avoid testing barriers that other groups were more willing to confront (Penrose 1980). Change-management was characterised by few clear objectives and little cohesion among management policy-makers. Reforms were prone to break down due to internal management conflict and poor co-ordination. This group often failed to generate a momentum for change. Typically, workrule reform was limited in scope and was confined largely to remedial measures sufficient to offset the crisis.

Conservative proceduralist

Generally, conservative proceduralist groups were more proactive than inert groups but tended to respond to long-term trends in the product market. This group strongly favoured traditional collective bargaining mechanisms and were suspicious of what they conceived to be 'fashionable' HRM practices. A broader scope for workrule change was detected, compared with inert groups, but conservative proceduralists were risk-averse and sought legitimacy for proposed changes through union endorsement. Their time horizon was oriented to long-term objectives, such as market share and sector dominance. Finally, these groups were characterised by incremental reform of substantive rules during the period of reference.

Consensual innovators

Like conservative proceduralists, this group was attuned to long-term product market developments. While retaining collective bargaining procedures, conservative innovators were knowledgeable about and favoured the introduction of 'soft', 'commitment–empowerment' HRM practices. A degree of opportunity to reform workrules was perceived but this was tempered by the desire to elicit change through employee consent. This group was unfavourably disposed towards confrontation of trade unions and employee groups and would typically seek to delay reforms in order to secure agreement but was ultimately prepared to impose change if necessary. Finally, the group was characterised by incremental procedural and substantive rule adjustment.

Aggressive proceduralists

Aggressive proceduralist groups reacted to short-term product market trends. This group preferred to route change through collective bargaining procedures, and were dismissive of innovations in personnel policy, such as HRM. They perceived a wide range of opportunities for workrule reform and were uncompromising in the way in which they negotiate change. This group adopted a high-risk position and was willing to countenance the possibility of labour hostility to their plans and resulting industrial action. Short-term profit maximisation characterised their objectives. The level of workrule reform was difficult to predict due to the higher possibility of their planned reforms being disrupted through organised resistance from employees.

Radical innovators

This group also responded primarily to short-term product market trends. Market changes were utilised to create a sense of continuing crisis. Typically favouring the introduction of 'hard' HRM, based upon the extension of personal contracts and individual appraisal, this group usually aimed to withdraw union collective bargaining rights. There was a heavy reliance of external advisers such as management consultants. As with the aggressive procedural group, this group perceived a broad range of opportunities for reform, and was unyielding in imposing its objectives. There was a focus upon short-term profit maximisation. Because this group adopted a high-risk strategy, the extent to which procedural and substantive workrules were reformed was difficult to predict.

A role for strategic choice?

Intense recession reduced the profitability of many panel firms, threatening the existence of many. This caused an initial wave of restructuring, aimed mainly at reducing firms' costs. Once product market conditions recovered, the external environment was characterised both by sharpened competitive pressures and by heightened economic uncertainty (Figure 8.1). The recession had ruptured expectations and few precedents were available for coping with the new, more competitive environmental context. Management had to contend with greater informational uncertainty, and with the need to make sense of equivocal product market cues. The power of the actual or potential enemy (i.e., labour) (Hyman 1987), to which managerial actions were directed, created a further element of insecurity.

This more unstable environment was filtered through managerial frames of reference. Policy-makers evolve an interpretative schema, constituted of broadly accepted norms and values, which is shaped by the group's history and internal politics, and by the corporate structure of the company in which the group is situated. The interpretative schema defined the 'width of agenda', or the range of options that were actively considered, and weighed which option was eventually adopted. Policy groups' frames of reference informed their reading of product market signals, their orientation towards collective bargaining institutions and emergent HRM policies, their perceived scope for manoeuvre in workplace relations, their change-management style and time horizon, and ultimately, the extent to which workrule change was secured and the nature of that change.

The core values and assumptions that are ingrained in policy-makers' interpretative schema may give rise to a 'closed loop' of mutually reinforcing choices. These may create a set of perceived barriers to opportunity, the limits of which are rarely overtly challenged. The outcome may be that frames of reference differ substantially from firm to firm, even between those companies trading in similar product markets and labour markets, and with comparable institutional characteristics. The present study discerned five types of interpretative framework. These were the inert, conservative procedural, conservative innovator, aggressive procedural and radical innovator. The effect was to refract broadly common competitive pressures through disparate interpretative media to produce a broad spectrum of workrule reform and a diverse pattern of change. Policy groups varied in their ability to sustain the impetus for change once the initial triggering event had subsided, and to translate any momentum into concrete procedural and substantive workrule reform.

This pattern of change cannot be satisfactorily accounted for by the strategic choice framework outlined in chapter 1. We noted that the dominant exposition, Kochan *et al.* (1986), states that a number of potential variables, including the external environment, actors' values, their history and current structures and their business strategies, may each influence the institutional structure of firm level industrial relations. But Kochan *et al.* say little about how these variables interact, and ultimately how choices come to be made. The present study has argued that management policy-

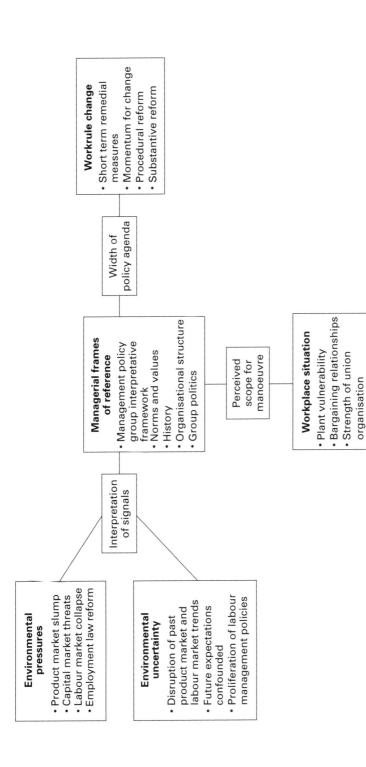

Figure 8.1 Competitive crisis, managerial frames of reference and reform of workrules

makers play an important role in interpreting and constructing their environment. They attach meaning to product market signals and weigh the scope for manoeuvre in workplace power relationships. The frames of reference of management policy-makers, which are closely interwoven with corporate structure and politics, define the 'width of agenda', or range of possibilities from which strategic choices are selected. Strategic choice is 'bounded' not merely by the available information (Cyert and March 1992: 214–15) but also by the perspective that policy-makers bring to the construction and processing of data. In certain cases, such as the 'inert' groups, a very limited range of choice was deemed to exist. At the opposite extreme, the 'aggressive proceduralist' and 'radical innovators' took an optimistic, perhaps unrealistic, view of what could be achieved.

This analysis leads away from a 'black box' view of management policy-making in industrial relations, in which external determinants act upon managerial actors. It directs attention towards the complex and sophisticated system of norms and rules which policy-makers create and reproduce, and which govern their own behaviour. This set of social rules is structured by the internal characteristics of the organisation and by its external environment. There has been a long history of ethnographic research which has looked closely at the behaviour of industrial workgroups. To date, there has been little comparable research into the dynamics of the management groups who are responsible for directing large corporations. Research in this area would benefit greatly from such a study.

References

Ahlstrand, B. (1990) *The Quest for Productivity: A Case Study of Fawley After Flanders* Cambridge: Cambridge University Press

Aldrich, H. (1979) *Organisations and Environments* Englewood Cliffs, NJ: Prentice Hall

Amason, A. C. (1996) 'Distinguishing the Effects of Functional and Dysfunctional Conflict on Strategic Decision Making: Resolving a Paradox for Top Management Teams' *Academy of Management Journal* 39, 1, 123–48

Bain, G. (1983) (ed.) *Industrial Relations in Britain* Oxford: Blackwell

Batstone, E., Ferner, A. and Terry, M. (1984) *Consent and Efficiency: Labour Relations and Management Strategy in the Public Enterprise* Oxford: Blackwell

Beer, M., Spector, B., Lawrence, P., Quinn Mills, D. and Walton, R. (1984) *Managing Human Assets* New York: The Free Press

Beyer, J., Chattopadhyay, P., George, E., Glick, W., Ogilvie, D. and Pugliese, D. (1997) 'The Selective Perception of Managers Revisited' *Academy of Management Journal* 40, 3, 716–37

Boland, R., Greenberg, R., Park, S. and Han, I. (1990) 'Mapping the Process of Problem Reformulation' in Huff, A. S. (ed.) *Managing Strategic Thought* New York: John Wiley

Brown, W. (1973) *Piecework Bargaining* London: Heinemann

(1981) *The Changing Contours of British Industrial Relations: A Survey of Manufacturing Industry* Oxford: Basil Blackwell

(1993) 'The Contraction of Collective Bargaining in Britain' *British Journal of Industrial Relations* 31, 2, 189–200

Brown, W. and Wadhwani, S. (1990) 'The Economic Effects of Industrial Relations Legislation Since 1979' *National Institute Economic Review* February, 57–70

Brown, W. and Walsh, J. (1991) 'Pay Determination in Britain in the 1980s: the Anatomy of Decentralization' *Oxford Review of Economic Policy* 7, 1

Brown, W., Deakin, S. and Ryan, P. (1997) 'The Effects of British Industrial Relations Legislation 1979–1997' *National Institute Economic Review* No. 161, July

Capelli, P. (1985) 'Competitive Pressures and Labor Relations in the Airline Industry' *Industrial Relations* 24, 3, 316–38

Capelli, P. and McKersie, R. B. (1987) 'Management Strategy and the Redesign of Work Rules' *Journal of Management Studies* 25, 5, 441–62

Child, J. (1972) 'Organisational Structure, Environment and Performance: The Role of Strategic Choice' *Sociology* 2–22

(1984) *Organization: A Guide to Problems and Practice* London: Paul Chapman Publishing

Child, J. and Smith, C. (1987) 'The Context and Process of Organisational Transformation – Cadbury Ltd in its Sector' *Journal of Management Studies* 24, 6, November, 565–93

Commission on Industrial Relations (1972) *Employers' Organizations and Industrial Relations* Study No. 1, London: HMSO

Cyert, R. and March, J. (1992) *A Behavioural Theory of the Firm* Blackwell: Oxford

Daniel, W. and Millward, N. (1983) *Workplace Industrial Relations in Britain* London: Heinemann

Davis, F. (1955) *Society and the Law* New York: Harper and Row

Deaton, D. (1985) 'Management Style and Large-Scale Survey Evidence' *Industrial Relations Journal* 16, 2, 67–71

Dickens, L. and Hall, M. (1995) 'The State: Labour Law and Industrial Relations' in Edwards, P. K. (ed.) *Industrial Relations: Theory and Practice in Britain* Oxford: Blackwell

Donaldson, G. and Lorsch, J. (1983) *Decision-Making at the Top: The Shaping of Strategic Direction* New York: Basic Books

Donovan, Lord (1968) *Royal Commission on Trade Unions and Employers' Associations* London: HMSO, Cmnd 3623

Dore, R. (1989) 'Where Are We Now: Musings of an Evolutionist' *Work, Employment and Society* 3, 4, 425–46

Dunn, S. (1979) 'Towards the End of Voluntarism in British Industrial Relations' Industrial Relations Department, London School of Economics

(1993) 'From Donovan to . . . Wherever' *British Journal of Industrial Relations* 31, 2, 169–87

Dunn, S. and Gennard, J. (1984) *The Closed Shop in British Industry* London: MacMillan

Dunn, S. and Metcalf, D. (1996) 'Trade Union Law Since 1979' in Beardwell, I. (1996) *Contemporary Industrial Relations: A Critical Analysis* Oxford: Oxford University Press, 66–98

Dunn, S. and Wright, M. (1993) 'Managing Without the Closed Shop' in Metcalf, D. and Milner, S. (eds.) *New Perspectives on Industrial Disputes* London: Routledge

(1994) 'Maintaining the Status Quo? An Analysis of the Contents of British Collective Agreements 1979–1990' *British Journal of Industrial Relations* 32, 1, 23–46

Dutton, J. E. and Duncan, R. B. (1987) 'The Creation of Momentum for Change Through the Process of Strategic Issue Diagnosis' *Strategic Management Journal* 8, 279–95

Eaton, A. and Voos, P. (1992) 'Unions and Contemporary Innovations in Work Organization, Compensation and Employee Participation' in Mishel, L. and Voos, P. B. (eds.), *Unions and Economic Competitiveness* Armonk, NY: Sharpe, 173–215

Edwards, P. K. (1987) *Managing the Factory: A Survey of General Managers* Oxford: Basil Blackwell

(1995a) 'The Employment Relationship' in Edwards (ed.) *Industrial Relations: Theory and Practice in Britain* Oxford: Blackwell

(1995b) (ed.) *Industrial Relations: Theory and Practice in Britain* Oxford: Blackwell

Elgar, J. and Simpson, R. (1992) 'The Impact of the Law on Industrial Disputes in the 1980s' Discussion Paper No. 104, Centre for Economic Performance: London School of Economics

Etzioni, A. (1961) *A Comparative Analysis of Complex Organisations* New York: Free Press

Evans, S. (1987) 'The Use of Injunctions in Industrial Disputes May 1984–April 1987' *British Journal of Industrial Relations* 25, 419–35

Ferner, A. (1988) *Governments, Managers and Industrial Relations* Oxford: Blackwell

Fernie, S. and Woodland, S. (1995) 'HRM and Workplace Performance Evidence Using WIRS3 – A Reply to McCarthy' *Industrial Relations Journal* 26, 1, 65–8

Fox, A. (1974) *Beyond Contract: Work, Power and Trust Relations* London: Faber

Freeman, R. and Pelletier, J. (1990) 'The Impact of Industrial Relations Legislation on British Trade Union Density' *British Journal of Industrial Relations* 28, 2, 141–64

Friedman, A. L. (1977) *Industry and Labour* London: Macmillan

Geary, J. (1995) 'Work Practices: The Structure of Work' in Edwards, P. K. (ed.) *Industrial Relations* Oxford: Blackwell

Glaser, B. and Strauss, A. (1968) *The Discovery of Grounded Theory* London: Weidenfeld and Nicolson

Goodrich, C. L. (1920: reprinted 1975) *The Frontier of Control: A Study in British Workshop Politics* London: Pluto Press

Gregg, P. and Yates, A. (1991) 'Changes in Wage Setting Arrangements and Trade Union Presence in the 1980s' *British Journal of Industrial Relations* 29, 361–76

Gregg, P., Machin, S. and Metcalf, D. (1993) 'Signals and Cycles? Productivity Growth and Changes in Union Status in British Companies 1984–1989' *Economic Journal* 103, 4, 894–907

Guest, D. (1991) 'Personnel Management: The End of Orthodoxy?' *British Journal of Industrial Relations* 29, 2, 149–76

Haley, U. C. and Stumpf, S. A. (1989) 'Cognitive Trails in Strategic Decision-Making: Linking Theories of Personalities and Cognition' *Journal of Management Studies* 26, 5, 477–97

Hill, S. (1981) *Competition and Control at Work* Aldershot: Gower

Janis, I. L. (1982) *Groupthink* Boston, MA: Houghton Mifflin

Kanter, R. M. (1984) *The Change Masters* London: Allen and Unwin

Keisler, S. and Sproull, L. (1982) 'Managerial Response to Changing Environments: Perspectives on Problem Sensing from Social Cognition' *Administrative Science Quarterly* 27, 548–70

Klein, J. (1991) 'A Re-examination of Autonomy in the Light of New Manufacturing Practices' *Human Relations* 44, 1, 21–38

Kochan, T., McKersie, R. B. and Capelli, P. (1984) 'Strategic Choice and Industrial Relations Theory' *Industrial Relations* 16–38

Kochan, T. A., Katz, H. and McKersie, R. B. (1986) *The Transformation of American Industrial Relations* New York: Basic Books

Layard, R. and Nickell, S. (1989) 'The Thatcher Miracle?' Discussion Paper No. 343, Centre for Labour Economics: London School of Economics

Loasby, B. J. (1976) *Choice, Complexity and Ignorance: An Enquiry into Economic Theory and the Practice of Decision-Making* Cambridge: Cambridge University Press

Lyles, M. A. and Thomas, H. (1988) 'Strategic Problem Formulation: Biases and Assumptions Embedded in Alternative Decision-Making Models' *Journal of Management Studies* 25, 2, 131–45

MacInnes, J. (1987) *Thatcherism at Work: Industrial Relations and Economic Change* Milton Keynes: Open University Press

Marchington, M. and Parker, P. (1990) *Changing Patterns of Employee Relations* Hemel Hempstead: Harvester Wheatsheaf

Marginson, P., Armstrong, P., Edwards, P. and Purcell, J. (1993) 'Decentralization, Collectivism and Individualism: Evidence on Industrial Relations in Transition from the 1992 Company Level Industrial Relations Survey' BUIRA Conference, July

Marginson, P., Edwards, P. K., Martin, R., Purcell, J. and Sisson, K. (1988) *Beyond the Workplace: Managing Industrial Relations in the Multi-Establishment Enterprise* Oxford: Basil Blackwell

Marginson, P., Olson, R. and Tailby, S. (1994) 'The Eclecticism of Management Policy Towards Labour Regulation' Warwick Paper in Industrial Relations No. 45, Industrial Relations Research Unit, Coventry

Marsh, A. (1982) *Employee Relations Policy and Decision-Making: A Survey of Manufacturing Companies Carried Out for the CBI* Aldershot: Gower

Mason, R. O. and Mitroff, I. I. (1981) *Challenging Strategic Planning Assumptions* New York: Wiley

McCarthy, W. E. J. (1964) *The Closed Shop in Britain* Oxford: Blackwell
    (1994) 'Of Hats and Cattle: Or the Limits of Macro-Survey Research in Industrial Relations' *Industrial Relations Journal* 25, 4, 315–22

Metcalf, D. (1989) 'Trade Unions and Economic Performance: The British Evidence' Discussion Paper No. 320, Centre for Labour Economics: London School of Economics
    (1993) 'Industrial Relations and Economic Performance' *British Journal of Industrial Relations* 31, 2, 255–83
    (1994) 'Transformation of British Industrial Relations? Institutions, Conduct and Outcomes 1980–1990' in Barrell, R. (ed.) *The UK Labour Market* Cambridge: Cambridge University Press

Millward, N. and Hawes, B. (1995) 'Hats, Cattle and IR Research: A Comment' *Industrial Relations Journal* 26, 1, 69–73

Millward, N. and Stevens, M. (1986) *British Workplace Industrial Relations 1980–84* Aldershot: Gower

Millward, N., Stevens, M., Smart, D. and Hawes, W. (1992) *Workplace Industrial Relations in Transition* Aldershot: Dartmouth

Mintzberg, H. (1978) 'Patterns in Strategy Formation' *Management Science* 24, 9, 934–48

Mintzberg, H., Raisinghani, P. and Theoret, A. (1976) 'The Structure of "Unstructured" Decision Processes' *Administrative Science Quarterly* 2, 246–75

Morris, T. and Wood, S. (1991) 'Testing the Survey Method: Continuity and

Change in British Industrial Relations' *Work, Employment and Society* 5, 2, 259–82

Nelson, R. and Winter, S. (1982) *An Evolution Theory of Economic Change* Cambridge, MA: Harvard University Press

Oulton, N. (1995) 'Supply Side Reform and UK Economic Growth. What Happened to the Miracle?' *National Institute Economic Review* November, 53–70

Pauuwe, J. (1991) 'Limitations to Freedom: Is there a Choice for Human Resource Management?' *British Journal of Management* 2, 103–19

Penrose, E. (1982) *The Theory of the Growth of the Firm* Blackwell: Oxford

Porter, M. E. (1980) *Competitive Strategy: Techniques for Analysing Industries and Competitors* New York: Free Press

Prahalad C and Bettis R (1986) 'The Dominant Logic: A New Linkage Between Diversity and Performance' *Strategic Management Journal* 7, 485–501

Purcell, J. (1987) 'Mapping Management Styles in Employee Relations' *Journal of Management Studies* 24, 5, 533–48

Purcell, J. and Sissons, K. (1983) 'Strategies and Practice in the Management of Industrial Relations' in Bain, G. (ed.) *Industrial Relations in Britain* Oxford: Blackwell

Purcell, J. and Ahlstrand, B. (1994) *Human Resource Management in the Multi-Divisional Company* Oxford: Oxford University Press

Reger, R. (1990) 'Managerial Thought Structures and Competitive Positioning' in Huff, A. S. (ed.) *Managing Strategic Thought* New York: John Wiley

Richardson, R. and Wood, S. (1989) 'Productivity Change in the Coal Industry and the New Industrial Relations' *British Journal of Industrial Relations* 27, 1, 33–56

Roethlisberger, F. J. and Dickson, W. J. (1939) *Management and the Worker* Cambridge, MA: Harvard University Press

Royal Commission on Trade Unions and Employers Associations (1965–8) *Report* London: HMSO

Schuler, R. S. and Jackson, S. (1987) 'Linking Competitive Strategies with Human Resource Management Practices' *Academy of Management Executive* 1, 3, 209–13

Schwenk, C. R. (1988) 'The Cognitive Perspective on Strategic Decision Making' *Journal of Management Studies* 25, 1, 41–55

(1989) 'Linking Cognitive, Organisational and Political Factors in Explaining Strategic Change' *Journal of Management Studies*, 26, 2, 177–87

Scott, A. (1994) *Willing Slaves? British Workers Under Human Resource Management* Cambridge: Cambridge University Press

Sisson, K. (1983) 'Employers' Organizations' in Bain, G. (ed.) *Industrial Relations in Britain* Oxford: Blackwell

(1989) 'Personnel Management in Perspective' in Sisson, K. (ed.) *Personnel Management in Britain* Oxford: Blackwell

(1993) 'Employers' Associations' in Bain, G. (ed.) *Industrial Relations in Britain* Oxford: Blackwell

(1993) 'In Search of HRM' *British Journal of Industrial Relations*, 31, 2, 201–10

Sisson, K. and Brown, W. (1983) 'Industrial Relations in the Private Sector:

Donovan Revisited' in Bain, G. (1983) (ed.) *Industrial Relations in Britain* Oxford: Blackwell

Sisson, K. and Marginson, P. (1995) 'Management: Systems, Structures and Strategy' in Edwards, P. K. (ed.) *Industrial Relations: Theory and Practice in Britain* Oxford: Blackwell

Smith, C., Child, J. and Rowlinson, M. (1990) *Reshaping Work: The Cadbury Experience* Cambridge: Cambridge University Press

Storey, J. (1980) *The Challenge to Management Control* London: Kogan Page
(1983) *Managerial Prerogative and the Question of Control* London: Routledge Kegan Paul
(1992) *Developments in the Management of Human Resources* Oxford: Blackwell
(1995) (ed.) *Human Resource Management: A Critical Text* London: Routledge

Storey, J. and Sisson, K. (1993) *Managing Human Resources and Industrial Relations* Milton Keynes: Open University Press

Storey, J., Ackers, P., Bacon, N., Buchanan, D., Coates, D. and Preston, D. (1994) *Human Resource Management Practices in Leicestershire: A Trends Monitor* Loughborough: Training and Enterprise Council/Loughborough University Business School

Walley, S. and Baum, J. R. (1994) 'Personal and Structural Determinants of the Pace of Strategic Decision Making' *Academy of Management Journal* 37, 4, 932–56

Walsh, J. (1993) 'Internalization v. Decentralization: An Analysis of Recent Developments in Pay Bargaining' *British Journal of Industrial Relations* 31, 3

Weick, K. (1979) *The Social Psychology of Organising* Reading, MA: Addison-Wesley

Whittaker, D. H. (1990) *Managing Innovation: A Study of British and Japanese Factories* Cambridge: Cambridge University Press

Whittington, R. (1993) *What is Strategy and Does it Matter?* London: Routledge

Index